Praise for the Original
ESSAYS THAT WORKED

"Outstanding."
The Journal of College Admissions

"For inspiration on what makes a
memorable essay, read *Essays That Worked*."
Money Magazine

"The best sort of teaching tool."
School Library Journal

"The collection reveals as much about the sorts of
students who are applying to college as about
the application process itself."
The Chronicle of Higher Education

Also published by Ballantine Books

ESSAYS THAT WORKED *for* **COLLEGE APPLICATIONS:**
50 Essays that Helped Students Get Into the Nation's Top Colleges

ESSAYS THAT WORKED *for* **LAW SCHOOLS:**
*40 Essays from Successful Applications
to the Nation's Top Law Schools*

ESSAYS THAT WORKED *for* **MEDICAL SCHOOLS:**
*40 Essays from Successful Applications
to the Nation's Top Medical Schools*

ESSAYS *That* WORKED®
for BUSINESS SCHOOLS

*40 Essays from Successful Applications
to the Nation's Top Business Schools*

REVISED AND UPDATED

Edited by
BOYKIN CURRY *and* **BRIAN KASBAR**

Revised by
EMILY ANGEL BAER

www.essaysthatworked.com

BALLANTINE BOOKS • NEW YORK

A Ballantine Book
Published by The Random House Publishing Group under license
from Mustang Publishing Co., Inc.
Copyright © 2003 by Mustang Publishing Co., Inc.

www.ballantinebooks.com

Library of Congress Catalog Card Number: 2003093357

ISBN 0-345-45043-4

Book design by Susan Turner

Manufactured in the United States of America

First Revised Edition: August 2003

10 9 8 7 6 5 4 3 2 1

ACKNOWLEDGMENTS

This book was created with the help of many students and admissions officers at some of the top business schools in America. We deeply appreciate the generosity of the applicants who let us reprint their essays and of the admissions officers who gave us their time, critiques, and advice.

We wish to extend our gratitude to David Webber at MIT, Eric Mokover at UCLA, Richard Silverman at Yale, Michelle Brown at Trinity University, and Diana Russell and Steve Denson at the Cox School of Business at Southern Methodist University.

Emily Angel Baer in particular thanks Tish Peterson for her comments, Eric Berman, and Ellis Haguewood for her comfortable office in which, on nights and weekends, she finished this project.

Boykin Curry

Brian Kasbar

Emily Angel Baer

For Roosevelt Evans, Joe Beckford, Walter A. Debboli Jr., and Bill Ohr
—men of Yale without whom this book would not have been possible.

And for the young men of Memphis University School
—students of today, leaders of tomorrow

CONTENTS

INTRODUCTION

How important is the essay on a business school application?

"To be honest, a person's record speaks much louder to us than his essay," one admissions officer told us.

"We give it quite a bit of weight," said another.

"It's at the heart of our entire process," said a third.

Along with your grades, your accomplishments, and, in some cases, your GMAT scores, the application essay can make the difference between your acceptance and rejection into an MBA program. For some schools, the essay is crucial. For others, it will only tip the balance of a borderline candidate.

After speaking with admissions officers at a number of business schools, we have tried to estimate just how important the essay is in the admissions process. The graph on page 2 shows our results. (Of course, the graph is in no way exact, and schools' attitudes can change with new deans and admissions officers, but it does roughly represent our understanding of the schools' current priorities.)

Also, note that several top business schools, particularly in the South, that have not required essays of past applicants are beginning to add them to their applications.

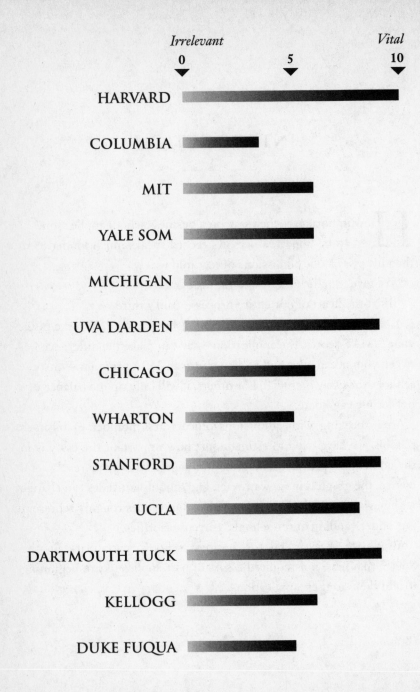

Irrelevant   Vital

0   5   10

HARVARD

COLUMBIA

MIT

YALE SOM

MICHIGAN

UVA DARDEN

CHICAGO

WHARTON

STANFORD

UCLA

DARTMOUTH TUCK

KELLOGG

DUKE FUQUA

Over the years, each of the top business schools has developed a distinct personality. Harvard, for example, has churned out one-fifth of the major officers at Fortune 500 companies, while Yale encourages students to make a contribution to the public sector. In response to these reputations, many students become chameleons in their applications. They are executives for Harvard, math jocks for MIT, and dedicated public servants for Yale.

Of course, admission officers usually see through that ploy quickly, and even if they don't, you're probably just hurting your application when you try to apply as someone you're not. Inconsistencies between your essays and your record are easy to spot; sentiment and expertise are tough to fake. The brochures for several business schools stress "general management," and one admissions officer told us that he is flooded with essays using the term "general manager" over and over in obsequious attempts to win a place. "It can become so repetitive," he said, "that I can't help but question the candidate's sincerity. The term has become meaningless."

Obviously, you should emphasize the parts of your personality and record that coincide with the school's interests. But avoid overdoing it. Be selective, but be yourself—it's the best sales pitch you can make.

In our book on undergraduate application essays, we discussed what kinds of content and tone were most appropriate in applying to college. Much of our advice holds true for business schools as well.

The overwhelming complaint from undergraduate admissions officers was that reading 13,000 essays on the same few topics in a span of three months is a mind-numbing experience. Most essays are dry and over-written. They are often "corrected" by so many friends and relatives that the life gets sucked out. One undergraduate admissions officer explained that "few applicants understand what we want to read, and they rarely go out on a limb to be witty or controversial." Anxious applicants become so afraid of saying the wrong thing that they end up saying nothing. Such sterilization can mean unbearable monotony for the hapless admissions staff, so don't treat your essay like a psychological minefield. What seems "safe" to you is probably deadly boring to a weary admissions officer.

The officer at one top school resorts to dramatic measures to combat essay fatigue. "I try to change the scenery when I read essays," he said. "I read them in the park or out on my boat. You know what? Even that doesn't help."

You can imagine, then, the impact that a lively, original essay can have. For starters, you are *noticed*, and that's much of the battle. But also, you have done a favor for the tired reader—and favors are often returned.

After reading the essays in this book, we hope you will understand better the boundaries of tone and content within which you can work, and we hope you see how large the boundaries are. Since these essays represent some of the best writing out of thousands of pieces submitted each year, they should inspire your creativity and help you feel more comfortable about the admissions process. As the essays demonstrate, you can be exciting and natural without resorting to outrageous gimmicks or immature poses. An accurate, enthusiastic reflection of your personality can make for a refreshing—and we hope successful—essay. Good luck!

AN INTERVIEW *with*
an ADMISSIONS OFFICER

Although different schools attach different levels of importance to the application essays, and although each school may be looking for a slightly different type of student, admissions officers have surprisingly similar desires. They want brevity. They want sincerity. They want mature enthusiasm. And a little humor—when it's truly humorous—doesn't hurt.

But as we perused the application questions and tried to compose our own answers, we found ourselves asking a number of questions. How "business-like" should we be? How much can we joke around? Can we relax and be the readers' chum, or should we treat them like clients? Should we tell them what they want to hear, or should we be totally honest, even at the risk of being boring?

We asked these and other questions to dozens of admissions officers at almost every major business school in the country. The following is a condensed version of those interviews:

What's the difference between application essays for business school and the essays we wrote to get into college?

The main difference is the way the author presents himself. What we ask of a college graduate is much more difficult than what colleges ask of a high school senior. And it should be. We don't want applicants to simply give a self-absorbed description of themselves, like they did for their college application. Rather, we want them to describe the world they see around them, and their place in it. An analogy we like to use around here is that with the essay, a student fashions a lens for us to view the world. From looking at the quality of that lens, we hope to judge the quality of its maker.

When we finish an essay, we expect to have learned something about the applicant and an industry or management or business. If an applicant has worked in a steel plant, for example, it should be interesting to see his understanding of the problems in the industry. What kind of management problems has he observed, and how would he change things? You can't expect that type of analysis from undergraduates.

We also expect more maturity for business school. That's partly a function of age—we're often dealing with people in their late 20's or 30's—but it's also an issue of direction. Undergraduates are coming to school to explore. It's hard to justify giving one of a few MBA spots to someone who is not pretty committed to a business career.

Do you want a description of a person or just his accomplishments?

We want an essay that brings the whole set of numbers into a coherent form. We want inconsistencies explained, and we want to see diverse activities as different facets of a single personality. We'd like to be able to say, "Oh, he did that, yeah, that makes sense. That fits with what we have." Both the performer and his track record should be discussed, so that we can know the person underneath all the accomplishments, and also how those activities affected that person.

An applicant could discuss, for example, how his jobs at a computer firm and at a wholesale food distributor will help him make grocery stores more efficient. Or how working in a defense firm led him to see the need for military procurement reforms.

Are there any hackneyed topics that applicants should avoid?

I would be lying if I said we dive enthusiastically into the drama of every investment banker's grueling program, but most of our questions are very personalized and no two people have exactly the same experience. Since we ask fairly specific questions, most answers are in the same vein, but we still get a good mix of ideas.

The similarity in topics is not what makes essays dull—and most of them certainly are. It's the monotonous style. Applicants tend to use too many big words and amorphous adjectives and not enough colorful details and observations.

If reading thousands of these essays is so boring, would you prefer that applicants try to entertain you?

First off, let me say that gimmicks do *not* work. This year we got an essay written in crayon on construction paper. It really hurt the applicant because it made us question his maturity and competence. That kind of joking might work occasionally for a college application, but we are dealing with much more sophisticated people at this level. Jokers are admitted only if their credentials are so good that we just can't refuse them.

You do have to captivate the reader somewhat, but many people hurt themselves by going too far. One applicant wrote an eight-page essay when we asked for one page. He was entertaining, but he didn't arrive at any point. And he didn't get very far in the admissions process, either. It's like marketing: get our attention and then *say something*. Just grabbing notice isn't enough.

I loathe "cute" essays. Nothing bugs me more than someone trying to be my funny pal. Dry wit is good, but when someone starts off with "Wow, investment banking is so neat," I just cringe.

I suppose my best advice is to write a mature essay—nothing too formal, though—and to integrate your personality into it as best you can. Don't be afraid to say what you feel. Remember that serious is not synonymous with humorless. We love wit, but it has to be backed up with meaningful points.

What about the offbeat essay? Does it have an advantage because it grabs your attention?

It's true that I get tired of the same self-descriptions of the thousands of people who apply here each year. We could fill our class ten times over with people from Wall Street, and it would be nice to see someone who is a bit "off beat." Given comparable work experience and success, I'd much rather take someone who has run a farm in Iowa than an investment banker.

But being off-beat just to get attention won't work. The uniqueness has to mesh with the rest of the application. We *do* want to see different facets of an applicant's personality. We *do* want people to show us how they differ from the other 7,000 applicants. But different doesn't mean outrageous. It can mean a New York consultant who takes ghetto kids camping on weekends, or a computer whiz with a passion for scuba diving. It does not mean some goofball just trying to impress us with a bunch of one-liners.

What advantage does a good writer have? Does style beat substance?

We try to be sensitive to poor writing skills, because we aren't looking for future authors or even scholars, necessarily. We're looking for future business leaders. We realize that engineers will be at a disadvantage when compared to advertisers, and we take that into account when we read the essays. But there's no question that writing style does make a difference. A good writer is convincing and engaging. She knows how to intrigue an audience, and she backs up her points with specific examples. Her ideas flow smoothly, and she makes the reader's job a lot easier. And if she is intelligent and witty, her essay is hard to forget.

Unfortunately, we get few essays of that caliber each year, and we won't hold it against you if you don't write a literary masterpiece. But we also keep in mind that skillful presentation and communication are crucial aspects of business.

If your readers want a good piece of advice when they start writing, let me say this: relax and just write. Only a small percentage of people bowl us over with style. What we really want is content.

One applicant wrote an essay wondering why people on death row always ask for a cigarette instead of writing down something about their lives or even making a last statement. Well, it's incredibly hard to express yourself, and we know that, so don't let your anxiety about style interfere with your need to write a meaningful essay.

So what are you looking for?

An honest, thoughtful essay. I know that sounds a little trite, but it's something we rarely see. Not only is that the best essay to read, but it should be the easiest to write. Concocting ridiculous anecdotes, attention-getting schemes, or a fictitious portrait is really a big waste of time and energy.

We want people to be vibrant, but we don't want gimmicks. We want a business-like approach, but we don't want to be fed dull, pompous lines.

Everyone wants us to give a recipe and a roadmap to the process, but what we want is someone who can navigate his own course. Within guidelines, of course.

SOME SAMPLE QUESTIONS

The following are essay questions and/or suggested topics from a variety of business school applications. Bear in mind that most B-school applications require several essays.

From Wharton:

Why did you decide to pursue management education? Looking ahead, what type of job would you expect or like to have five **and** ten years after receiving your master's degree? What is your ultimate career objective? In realizing these goals, do you foresee your career as a business leader having an impact on society at large?

What do you consider to have been your single most significant achievement to date?

From Kellogg:

What is the most challenging problem that you have faced, and how have you solved it?

You have been selected as a member of the Admissions Committee. Please provide a brief evaluative assessment of your file.

From Stanford:

Describe an ethical dilemma that you have personally encountered. What alternative actions did you consider and why? Do **not** tell us what you decided to do.

From the University of Michigan:

There is a lot of controversy over the usefulness of the MBA. What do you consider to be the strengths and weaknesses of the degree?

From Dartmouth:

What are your principal interests outside of your job or school? Why do they appeal to you?

From Harvard:

Given your experience with your current employer (or school you attend) and given the opportunity to effect one change, what would that be? How would you implement the change?

Do you feel your academic history is indicative of your ability to succeed at Harvard Business School? Why or why not? If not, please support with additional evidence of your academic ability.

From Southern Methodist University:

Describe a recent accomplishment that demonstrates your potential for a successful management career.

Write an article that would be published about yourself in eight to ten years from now.

From Duke:

Please discuss your previous professional experiences, your long-term career goals, and the role the MBA will play in those plans. What do you hope your contribution will be to an MBA environment?

From MIT's Sloan School:

The statement of objectives is your opportunity to describe your reasons for wanting to do graduate work in management at the Sloan School. . . . We have not posed specific questions for you, preferring that you determine which aspects of your background and aspirations are relevant to your application.

From UCLA:

Write your own essay question and answer it. Take a risk.

Discuss a situation, preferably work-related, where you have taken a significant leadership role. How does this event demonstrate your managerial potential? (Limit to one page.)

USING—*and* ABUSING—*the* INTERNET

The admissions officer is sitting at his desk, piles of papers everywhere indicating the degree to which he is overworked (or perhaps his own relaxed approach to organization). He is reading the forty-ninth essay of the day, when suddenly he has a wave of *déjà vu*.

Now, he's been reading admissions essays at his private business school for five years, and he's often read essays that remind him of something else. But this one—hmmmm:

New Albany City, check. Time, 15:30. Great! Reset timer; power normal; oil temperature, within range; compass setting, correct. Alone at 4,000 feet in a small airplane in a strange new territory and I am piloting my way perfectly. I feel like Lindbergh!

Is it possible that he's read about two student pilots this year? Coincidence? He thinks not. He reads through the essay about this young man's euphoric first solo flight and becomes more convinced that he has seen it before. He shuffles through the applications that he placed in a stack for a second review.

Bingo! There it is—the same essay in an application from two weeks ago. Punctuation, paragraphing, wording, all exactly the same. He glances through the application. One recommendation mentions the flying lessons; the other one does not. Both applicants come from large urban areas, but not the same urban area—not even the same state. Both are bright and tech savvy. Their undergraduate transcripts and their work histories indicate a big interest in the Internet. In fact, one employer recommendation names the computer as the culprit when the applicant missed deadlines or came to meetings unprepared. She intended to praise his expertise and thoroughness, but now the admissions officer is reading between the lines.

Taking a welcome break, he begins to surf the net himself and quickly finds several Web sites that offer help for grad school application essays. He subscribes to a few of the larger sites and finds one that will provide an essay of your choice on a variety of topics—for a fee, naturally. Thirty minutes later, he finds the exact essay the applicants submitted.

Both students are quickly rejected, of course. Furthermore, the admissions officer "unofficially" alerts his colleagues at the other MBA programs listed on the students' GMAT reports. It seems unlikely that either student will attend the business school of his choice.

While this example is a compilation of several stories, the tale of the duplicate essay is absolutely true. Any dishonesty in connection with the application will prevent your admission to business school. If cheating is discovered after you've been accepted (and in one incident at Stanford, after a student had started classes), your acceptance will be rescinded.

While blatant plagiarism is rare, "canned" essays are becoming common. Increasingly, admissions officers are seeing the "packaging" of applicants. What has made this unhappy trend grow is the use—and abuse—of the Internet.

In one random search, we found almost a thousand Web sites "guaranteeing" a winning application essay—college, law school, business school, dental school, you name it. One service offers a "final polish of the essay." This same site adds: "Unlike other sites, our editors do not merely write a critique of your essay; instead, they actually correct and make changes to your essay while maintaining your unique voice."

This claim is, by definition, impossible; if your voice is unique, how can "they" duplicate it? "They" don't even know you!

Another service is even more blatant. Their Web site states: "We draft your university, graduate, or professional school essays or college admissions statements from the information you provide to us." Another one simply asks for your bio, and they take it from there. Be aware that, while admissions readers are looking for your own voice, they're also pretty good at detecting when it's *not* there. They want to see how you express yourself. As one admissions director said, "When that expression becomes a product of someone else's work, there's a word for that: *plagiarism.*"

The price for a graduate school application essay starts at $500, depending on how much assistance you receive and how fast you want it. The sites generally tout readers from schools such as Harvard, Yale, and Stanford, though there's no way to prove they have any affiliation with those schools—and chances are, they don't. Other sites are run by independent counselors (in one case, a mother who honestly admits she's just selling advice from her home) who charge fees for services that are provided free at most colleges and on many legitimate Web sites.

While many sites are entirely honest, the Internet has provided almost unlimited possibilities for fraud. But you'll find that it's hard to deceive a good admissions officer. They've been trained; they've read hundreds of essays before yours; and they know at least as much about the Web as you do.

In fact, several Web sites, such as Plagiarized.com, help readers determine whether an essay is genuine, and there's software available specifically for detecting copied papers. Is it foolproof? Of course not. But is buying an essay off the Web a risk worth taking? Aside from the immorality of it, look at the practical aspect: If you submit a bad essay, it alone probably won't get you rejected. If you submit a plagiarized essay and it's discovered, you're immediately rejected—at that school, and probably at every school to which you've applied.

Of course, cheating is not new, and it won't disappear. The Internet simply offers enticing new ways to lure even the best students into thinking they *need* an essay service, when, in reality, it's the last thing they need. None of the essays in this book are Pulitzer Prize winners, but they are honest products of the students. When an essay isn't genuine, an admissions officer can smell it, and the results can be disastrous. And no one, no matter how desirable, is immune to close scrutiny on the essay. An admissions officer at Stanford recently said, "We just turned down an incredible prospect; the essays killed him." He went on to say that Stanford is seeing too much "editing" on student essays—sometimes the result of an overzealous school counselor, more often due to the growing influence of Internet sources.

An admissions officer from a private school in Georgia wrote:

I had a case this year of a kid who stole an essay off the Internet and tried to pass it off as his own. It sounded familiar but I couldn't put my finger on it. I posted something on the NACAC [National Association for College Admissions Counseling] *Web site and within ten minutes people had sent me five or six sources. . . . By the way, I wrote a deny letter to him and sent a duplicate to his parents.*

The Internet can provide terrific, legitimate suggestions and tips for all aspects of the application process, including the essay. The best place to start is at the business school's site itself. You can access any graduate school on-line by using the university's name, generally followed by ".edu." Read as much about the university as you can, including the questions they ask on their application. Familiarize yourself with whatever is unique about a specific institution. Ask yourself, "Why do I want to go to Takemeplease School of Business?" If you can answer that question, you can probably write a good essay.

Many Web sites are excellent sources for all kinds of university and admissions data. For example, www.collegeboard.com (associated with the College Board, which is more than a hundred years old) has useful information about all aspects of the process, including preparing for the GMAT, applying on-line, writing the essay, getting financial aid, and even choosing the school that's right for you.

The National Association for College Admissions Counseling (www.nacac.com) has great advice and links to other information sources, including essay help. Yahoo! offers several free services, some of which you must register for, such as GMAT tips and preparation, on-line applications, college searches, and financial aid.

The bottom line: Almost any information you want is available free on the Internet. But be careful, because the Internet alone can't get you through the application process. Not everything you see on the Internet is valid or germane to your experience.

According to the NACAC, more students are applying on-line every year. Critics say that some schools encourage on-line applications just to increase the number of applications they receive. This way, their well-publicized rejection rates will seem higher. Whether or not this is the case, it is a fact that the majority of universities today provide admission applications on-line. Some even have applications available on-line *only*. Remember that all electronic resources begin with what you yourself contribute. There is still no substitute for self-discovery. What motivates you in your choice of B-schools: Location? Reputation? Accessible professors? Class size? Career guidance? What is significant about the particular school you wish to attend? How does it seem right for you? The more you know about yourself, the more useful on-line information can be.

One senior admissions officer wrote: "As students become increasingly Internet savvy, I think we will be experiencing a rise in those who are willing to apply on-line." As on-line applications increase, there will be more access to on-line aids—both honest and dishonest—for the application essays. The trick is to recognize the difference between helpful hints and outright cheating. Make your essay authentic. To be authentic, you should not sound like a forty-year-old editor.

Your own voice is your best chance of showing an admissions officer that you are special and that you belong at his or her school.

Most of the on-line services for graduate school essays charge a fee, but these sites often provide helpful hints in their free material. The following is an excellent "Do's and Don'ts" list from Accepted.com:

The Do's

- Unite your essay and give it direction with a theme or thesis. The thesis is the main point you want to communicate.

- Before you begin writing, choose what you want to discuss and the order in which you want to discuss it.

- Use concrete examples from your life experience to support your thesis and distinguish yourself from other applicants.

- Write about what interests you, excites you. That's what the admissions staff wants to read.

- Start your essay with an attention-grabbing lead—an anecdote, quote, question, or engaging description of a scene.

- End your essay with a conclusion that refers back to the lead and restates your thesis.

- Revise your essay at least three times.

- In addition to your editing, ask someone else to critique your personal statement for you.

- Proofread your personal statement by reading it out loud or reading it into a tape recorder and playing back the tape.

- Write clearly, succinctly.

The Don'ts

- Don't include information that doesn't support your thesis.

- Don't start your essay with "I was born in . . . ," or "My parents came from. . . ."

- Don't write an autobiography, itinerary, or résumé in prose.

- Don't try to be a clown (but gentle humor is OK).

- Don't be afraid to start over if the essay just isn't working or doesn't answer the essay question.

- Don't try to impress your reader with your vocabulary.

- Don't rely exclusively on your computer to check your spelling.

- Don't provide a collection of generic statements and platitudes.

- Don't give mealymouthed, weak excuses for your GPA or test scores.

- Don't make things up.

There are other helpful Web sites as well. The following list can give you great advice and food for thought as you prepare to write your personal statement. Check them out, but use judiciously:

www.mbastrategies.com

www.princetonreview.com/mba/apply

www.accepted.com/mba

www.studentaffairs.columbia.edu/preprofessional

www.petersons.com/mba

www.kaptest.com

www.usnews.com/usnews/edu/grad/rankings/mba/
    mbaindex_brief.php

The Internet is an enticing tool, but there's no substitute for simply reading real essays from real people. Take a hint from the examples collected here: Be yourself, whatever that may be. You're a college graduate, you've probably already worked full-time, maybe you already have a family, and your specific goal is to become a better manager or executive or entrepreneur or whatever. Dilbert jokes aside, you have chosen an exciting, demanding course of study. Take a risk. Let your essay show your potential for growth, for contemplating new ideas, for change. Above all, be honest—to yourself, to your potential business school, and to your own future.

THE ESSAYS

For organizational purposes only, we divided the essays into eight groups: Essays that Discuss Strengths and Weaknesses, Ethical Essays, Essays About Work Experiences, Essays About the MBA, Essays About Accomplishments, Extracurricular Essays, *Personal* Personal Statements, and Offbeat Essays. Please bear in mind that this grouping is totally artificial. In fact, there is some overlap of topics; in some cases, an essay we placed in one category might fit just as well in another. You don't need to write an essay that would fit neatly into one of these categories. You do have to write an essay that attempts to answer the question, and most business school applications require several essays, not just one.

We created the introductions to each grouping based on our own research and on comments from admissions officers and other admissions counselors. More than ever, applicants to B-school have had a variety of work experiences, and some of the essays collected here reflect unusual and/or outstanding opportunities students had before even considering an MBA. Your own experience may pale by comparison, at least in your mind. Nevertheless, the models provided here can help you see how to state your case with clarity and precision. Also, although we think these are excellent models, they are not perfect. Each essay represents one part of an application that probably asked for four or five essays. We urge you, then, to read all of the essays. If you do, you'll be in great shape to compose your own application package.

Of course, the questions themselves will probably limit your range of responses. When you applied to college, you most likely had one vague, open-ended topic, such as "Write a brief essay that describes who you are." Application essay topics for graduate school tend to be more specific. For example, UCLA has asked, "Discuss two or three situations in the past three years where you have taken a leadership role. How do these events demonstrate your managerial potential?" Although your answer to a topic like that must be structured, you will still have a great opportunity to present a unique, memorable, even imaginative image.

The essays that follow are reproduced almost exactly as they were submitted, though of course the typeface and spacing are different. In some cases, minor spelling or grammatical errors have been corrected, but rarely would such correction be needed for a successful essay. In this collection, we had some favorites from our past editions that remain great examples of successful essays. In those, we took the liberty of removing certain references to dates.

Since most of the authors requested anonymity, we have deleted some proper names and sometimes substituted a more general name in place of a specific reference. In addition, at the request of a few schools, we sometimes disguised the name of the school to which the writer applied. However, our substitutions never distort the intent of the author.

Read Them All

Let's get one thing straight: The essays in this book are not standards that you have to meet in order to get into business school. Some of you might have essays in your head far better than anything here. (If so, let us read them! See **www.essaysthatworked.com** for information on submitting your essays for the next edition of this book.) These are simply essays that worked, not the *only* essays that worked.

We hope that you will first read all the essays. There's a wide range here; some are 500 words, some are 5,000. Some have dialogue, some are aggressive, some are reflective. The question you should ask yourself as you read is not, "Is this a good essay?" but rather, "Do I get to know this writer from this essay?" If you are an admissions officer, you will also ask, "Now that I know this applicant, does he/she match my school?"

Getting into B-school is not a writing contest; the competition is more subtle than that. More important than how well you write is how well you illustrate who you are and whether a particular school is right for you. Believe it or not, the admissions officer wants what's best for you. With the ever-increasing quality of the applicant pool, most schools have little trouble filling their first-year classes. Your task is to communicate something new and meaningful about yourself to someone who knows you only by your numbers.

A Warning

While we know that no one would be foolish enough to copy any of these essays verbatim, some of you might be tempted to take an essay and "change it around a little" to suit your application. We hope you know how stupid that would be. For one thing, stealing a phrase or even an idea from an essay in this book is flat-out dishonest. Duke University, the University of Virginia, and many other schools maintain that the application is covered by their Honor Codes. Thus, cheating on the application will guarantee your rejection from those schools. In fact, Stanford recently expelled a student two months into the academic year when they discovered he had plagiarized his application essay.

Remember, this has been a popular book for many years. Most admissions officers have read this book and are familiar with each essay. No admissions officer would ever admit a plagiarist.

A counselor from a prestigious prep school sent us this anecdote regarding *Essays that Worked for College Applications:*

When I was Associate Dean of Admissions at Georgetown in the [late '80s], we were asked to select memorable essays from among the applications of students who were being admitted. Two enterprising Yale graduates had requested samples of "essays that worked" to publish in a guidebook aimed at a high school audience. Because of our involvement in the project, we received several complimentary copies of the volume, which I read out of curiosity.

This background knowledge proved useful during my tenure on the George Washington University admissions staff in a subsequent year. Imagine my surprise when I reviewed an application, only to recognize one of the examples from Essays That Worked. *Although the student had elaborated on the original theme, the initial paragraph was word for word part of an essay that appeared in the book.*

The student who plagiarized was unequivocally denied, even though he would normally have been a good candidate. Instead of increasing his chances of admission, he instantly destroyed the value of all his academic achievements over three and a half years. I shared with his college counselor the reason for our decision, knowing that the message would be relayed to the student. What a shame! He didn't trust his own ability to be impressive enough.

The following pages demonstrate the creative potential of the business school application essay. We hope these essays will inspire you when you begin to write, and we hope they will give you the confidence to write a bold, personal piece that is truly your own and that will help an admissions officer see why you are special. Enjoy the essays, study them, and let them be a catalyst for your own creativity.

ESSAYS THAT DISCUSS
STRENGTHS *and* WEAKNESSES

O ne essay theme concerns your strengths and weaknesses, although this topic more often comes up in the interview. The
subject can be a proxy for many subtler questions: Are you arrogant?
Do you lack self-confidence? Do you understand yourself—or do you
just *think* you do? Are you honest and forthright, or a little too
shrewd and manipulative?

A common response among successful writers is to offer a broad
but observable strength backed by anecdotal evidence. Colorful examples that illustrate your strengths can be quite engaging, and they
allow you to make your point strongly without bragging. But watch
out if you find yourself using a lot of adjectives and just a few verbs.
No one wants someone who talks a lot and acts a little. If you have
many strengths, make sure you are *exhibiting* them, not just describ-
ing them.

Analytic ability and interpersonal skills are essential to business and
life. Be sure to demonstrate some talent in these areas.

As for weaknesses, we observed an increasing trend: The best weaknesses were usually strengths in disguise. "I work too hard" is a common refrain. "I'm impatient with those less intelligent than myself"
is another. While these "positive weaknesses" are often legitimate
and require attention, they are usually just strengths in excess. Such
"weaknesses" can label a writer as insincere and sly.

Not one successful essay we read described a weakness of character, motivation, or intelligence, such as "I lie sometimes," "I get bored at work," or "I have trouble keeping up." Studies of high-level business people reveal that many feel like frauds, that they believe they hold positions they don't deserve. Among successful applicants, however, this type of weakness is rarely discussed.

We're not advising you to conceal the truth and write a contrived essay. If your grades are mediocre, don't try to convince the admissions officers that you were "too driven" in school. But this is one question that demands a delicate touch. Would Harvard rather spend resources on someone who is "always late to work" or someone who is a self-proclaimed "workaholic"? All things being equal, the workaholic wins.

With good writing, you can describe real weaknesses without sounding bitter or pathetic. Think about yourself for a few days. Spend an hour writing stories that display your faults. Don't be inhibited or strategic—be brutal. This exercise is interesting and not too painful, and it will give you an accurate, honest foundation for your essay.

Then be discreet.

A word of caution: This essay question is not found on many applications. If it is included in a choice of topics, avoid it. From the many essays we read, we found that the "strengths and weaknesses" essays are the least effective. If you address the other essay questions with candor and detail, the reader will see your strengths in action. It requires creativity to produce a really good essay about weaknesses that can still promote you as a candidate for a treasured spot in a high-level MBA program.

WHAT IS YOUR GREATEST WEAKNESS?

Here's a sample of the brutal, wrenching self-criticism found in a few essays. Bear in mind that most admissions officers place such phrases in the Give-Me-a-Break Department.

My greatest weakness is:

". . . my tendency to over-research topics when time is available."

". . . that I do not like to waste time."

". . . that I expect as much out of others as I do out of myself."

". . . that sometimes people confuse what I have to say to them."

". . . that I'm too much of a leader."

Motivation and creativity are two strengths I could contribute to the community at [your business school]. As my academic and employment histories will attest, I am an extremely motivated individual. As an undergraduate, I enrolled in extra units and graduated a semester early. As a professional, I advanced from a light staff to a heavy staff nine months ahead of the normal progression, and I attribute this demonstration of drive and energy as the primary factor in securing employment as a management consultant. Regarding creativity, the problem-solving orientation of consulting requires a high degree of creativity and imagination. I have demonstrated my abilities by creating new and unique approaches and solutions.

A characteristic I am attempting to improve is my self-confidence. As a new consultant, I have tried to overcome the credibility barrier to develop the effective interchange necessary to provide quality counsel. The task has proven to be difficult. Working with associates holding MBA's from the top business schools and advising senior executives with more years of business experience than my age is unnerving. However, the interaction demanded [by your] case method will, without doubt, build my self-esteem and confidence.

The attribute that has contributed most to my career as a journalist is my ability to analyze complex and fast-changing situations, no matter how unfamiliar or specialized the subject matter. Because of my reputation for quick learning and flexibility, I often have been assigned by my editors to cover emergency situations and complicated subject matters—from corporate takeovers and complex investigative stories, to natural disasters and guerrilla warfare. And I have repeatedly proven my ability to cover these stories under the extreme competitive pressures of a daily newspaper.

I have learned to spot key trends amid masses of seemingly unrelated information. My employer demands analytical and thoughtful coverage from its reporters, forcing me to look beyond superficial news events to find the underlying causes or to predict future developments.

An important tool in this process is my ability to communicate. Obviously, my ability to express myself in writing has been vital. Just as important, however, is the skill in personal communications I have developed to cajole information from reluctant news sources or negotiate my way through hazardous situations. While relentless in fulfilling my responsibilities to gather information, I believe I know how to do so without falling prey to the over-aggressiveness often ascribed to journalists.

And, to present controversies in a balanced manner, I've relied on my natural ability to get along with a wide variety of news sources. I have learned to delve into the motivations of people totally unlike myself, putting aside my own biases to absorb the views of others. At the same time, when the facts support harsh judgments and conclusions, I have been willing to withstand extreme pressures and criticism that result from controversial articles.

Moreover, I've proven adept at working by myself for extended periods of time and then blending easily into teams of reporters and editors. On several occasions I've been assigned to team projects because of my ability to help coordinate groups of highly individual journalists who otherwise couldn't, or wouldn't, work together.

A weakness I've worked to correct is my tendency to over-research topics when I have the time available. I have occasionally let my natural curiosity, and my drive to ensure that I have adequate information to support my published conclusions, lead me too deeply into research projects. I have recognized this problem, however; I believe my accomplishments show that for the most part I have been able to balance the need to work efficiently with my responsibility to thoroughly report information for my stories.

If I were to read this application as an admissions officer, my greatest concern about the individual in question would be a depth of character and experience that might not yet have developed in a person of my age. Whenever I read a resume or application of a young "fast track" professional, I question the one-dimensionality that all too frequently characterizes bright, ambitious but otherwise shallow achievers. Were I involved in the admissions process, I would make every effort to admit individuals who are highly motivated and performance-oriented; that fact notwithstanding, however, I would also seek those individuals who possess the intangible yet compelling personal attributes that are distilled from a wealth of tangibly unique experiences.

After an in-depth reading of this application, I form a mental image of a 24-year-old, bright, inquisitive challenge-seeker who possesses a natural bent for the appreciation of foreign cultures and a fascination with global issues. At an age where none of the truly formidable crossroads of life have yet been met, might not this person expand her intellectual horizons in a more unrestricted manner, for example, by apprenticing as a wine-taster in one of the great French wine châteaux? Or studying art history and language at the Sorbonne? Or even experimenting with hidden talents at the culinary schools of La Varenne or La Notre in Paris? Why isn't this applicant studying political science in an Eastern Bloc university, journeying by train across Russia, sailing up the Yellow River on a barge excursion or trekking through the Himalayas of Nepal? For a motivated, resourceful individual, the scope of uniquely enriching cultural opportunities is unlimited: archaeological digs in the Andes, rough water sailing off Australia, an internship on the Senate Foreign Affairs Committee, or set design for a theater on Broadway. It is evident that the individual described herein possesses a surfeit of qualifications, talent and practical experience. In the final analysis, however, the question is one of whether the individual also possesses the diversity of lessons, both the everyday and the unusual, the exciting and the mundane, that ordinary life (in many not-so-ordinary places) has to offer.

Why do I believe that you will overrule the consideration expressed in this essay? The answer is the following: I believe that an individual who realizes the need for depth of character forged by unrestricted intellectual exploration is a long way along the road to acquiring that sought-after depth. And I am enough of an optimist to believe that I can juggle business school and a concurrent diversity of experiences that will allow me to progress the rest of the way down that road.

My mother is a Buddhist; my father, a Baptist. My mother was the only daughter of a wealthy elite Korean family who gave her the best of all the social and educational advantages. My father was the fifth son of a poor uneducated family from Virginia who sent him on his way to work for the U.S. Army in Korea. When my mother married my father, she was completely disinherited and was never allowed to see her family again. The legacy of difficult choices and the blending of two diverse cultures have had a unique impact on my character and my perspective on life.

I made a choice at an early age to be strong. When I was seven months old, I contracted a virus which the local Korean doctor diagnosed as flu. It turned out to be polio. From the example set by my mother to marry my father despite all odds, I realized that I too could accomplish anything I wanted to do in life. Thus, I have developed a reservoir of enormous inner strength. I set high standards for myself and I am, perhaps, tougher on myself than anyone else. Having polio is like having a ready-made excuse for any failure. I made the choice not to believe in excuses.

Because of my determination to succeed, I have been enthusiastic about life and all that it has to offer. I am curious, open-minded, adventuresome, and somewhat daring. While in Korea, I was the President of the Junior Travel and Culture Club and I organized trips throughout Korea and Japan. I have ventured into the depths of majestic, multi-colored caves and I have hiked up mountains to see Buddhist statues carved into stone walls. I have even led a group of students to Panmunjum, the military demarcation of North and South Korea. I once stepped over the boundary into North Korea only to be suddenly circled by twelve well-armed North Korean guards. I told them that I was just testing them out.

As a student leader and a collegiate debator at USC, I have traveled extensively throughout the United States. Many times I have competed at debate tournaments during winter in the east coast or in the mid-west. It may have taken me longer to get my briefcases to the next debate round while plowing through several inches of snow, but I had the distinct advantage of having more time to think about my debate strategy. When I traveled to Washington, D.C. to speak out on financial aid and tuition issues, other student leaders remembered me and I was able to successfully organize a national letter-writing campaign against the proposed federal financial aid cuts.

Initiative and independence have characterized my life. My family moved to a rural farming community atop the Ozark Mountains when I was 16 years old. There were more cows than people there. I knew that I wasn't meant to be Rebecca of Sunnybrook Farm so when I graduated from high school, I moved to San Francisco and found an apartment and a job on my own. It was this same independence that has compelled me to finance my undergraduate education by winning several scholarships and working full- and part-time during school.

I am continually learning to balance my fierce independence with my strong belief in the worth of others. Having lived in such diverse places as Seoul (Korea), Arkansas, San Francisco, and Los Angeles, I have come to appreciate the differences and similarities among seemingly incompatible cultures. I am perceptive and sensitive. Perhaps this is the result of the skills I had to develop at an early age. As a child, I quickly learned that people did not necessarily mean what they said. Ironically, instead of being helped by others, I found myself in a role of making others comfortable relating to a child who had polio.

The synthesis of my unique background and my understanding of other people has resulted in others perceiving me to be a leader with a tremendous amount of energy, perserverence, and integrity. People believe in me. At USC, I convinced the student government to take tough stands on academic standards and to fight for more student services. I am most comfortable in a leadership position, and at the same time, I must balance this with my belief in teamwork. I don't want to be so strong that I subjugate the weak; rather, I want to inspire others to be strong. When I believe in something, I am passionate, enthusiastic, and driven. I have the ability to communicate this belief and commitment to others to an extent that both surprises and humbles me.

I believe I communicate effectively with small and large groups. While [a member of the student government] at USC, I especially enjoyed making presentations and speeches before student groups, administrators, and the Faculty Senate. I had the reputation of being able to move a crowd to tears, although this always seemed to happen when I told a joke.

Debating has further sharpened my verbal and analytical skills. I have learned to think on my feet, to defend a position, and to attack cases. I remember one particular round in which my partner and I were debating a team of young men from an eastern school. Their opening arguments ended with innuendos about the inadequacy of women to debate. Aside from being an ad hominem argument, I realized that it was a personal attack since there are very few female collegiate debators. I looked at my partner and said, "Let's kill 'em." We did.

I am learning to evaluate whether I would like to debate or to persuade. I have won more arguments on a personal level by weakening my position, yet I have the ability, and many times desire, to over-kill an argument. I want to learn to become passionate about the right issues and to distinguish those from irrelevent ones.

My strengths have developed out of my weaknesses and my weaknesses may come out of my strengths. Weaknesses many times result from not knowing when to subdue strengths. I am learning to achieve a balance between the two. By synthesizing my skills, I am increasing the range of strengths that I can use in appropriate circumstances. As a manager, this is important, for I know there will be a time to speak out and a time to listen, a time to lead and a time to follow, and a time to be confident and a time to be humble.

Giving an evaluation of yourself is always difficult, but I believe those people that are candid about themselves and truly understand their strengths and weaknesses will be the most successful. My two greatest strengths are self-confidence and determination. I do not believe in negative thinking, and am confident that I can accomplish whatever I set my mind to. I am ambitious and believe I am a natural leader through my ability to express myself and organize people and things. I like to be given responsibility because I believe I have good judgment, and I like to make decisions quickly.

My weaknesses are in large part connected to my strengths. My most glaring weakness is my impatience. I am a person who does not like to waste time, nor do I like to wait. My impatience sometimes gets me in trouble with people when they are slower at performing a task than I. I often find myself apologizing in these situations. Another weakness of mine is that I am occasionally too bossy. Often when I am involved in an activity I will try to take up a leadership role and delegate responsibility, which sometimes unnerves people. I do not do this purposely, but I frequently am able to analyze a situation quicker than most, and then I act on impulse. My last weakness is that I can seem overbearing. When I go full steam into a project I want everyone around me to share my enthusiasm for that project. If they do not, they may find my zest to get the project completed abrasive or overbearing.

ETHICAL ESSAYS

In a speech on the "Psychology of Risk, Speculation, and Fraud," novelist and former banker Linda Davies said, "Bankers who hire money-hungry geniuses should not always express surprise and amazement when some of them turn around with brilliant, creative, and illegal means of making money."

Ivan Boesky may be old news, but names like Martin Frankel, Robert Maxwell, Bernie Ebbers, Kenneth Lay, and Richard Scrushy continue to be the stuff of articles and investigations. One recent survey discovered that 56 percent of workers feel some pressure to act unethically or illegally on the job. As businesses recognize the impact of legal and ethical lapses on their employees and customers, business schools have become increasingly concerned about the ethical standards of the leaders they will graduate. Many applications now require students to discuss an ethical dilemma, and these essays can be tougher than you think.

Don't congratulate yourself for being always honest because, honestly, you aren't. White lies, exaggerations, misconstructions, and such are part of everyone's social routine. If you glibly write, "I never lie," you will reveal more about your personality than you realize. On the other hand, don't cynically ponder how easy it would be to have taken "the other route." Such a tack makes you at the least a martyr and at the worst a potential crook.

Instead, approach the ethical essay with honest realism. Write briefly about the responsibilities you believe in, and then discuss how you have upheld certain principles. You need to show that, as an intelligent, educated person, you are willing to pay a price for high ethical standards. But be careful not to overdo it, because hokey insincerity is obvious and devastating. Discuss something you truly care about, even if your story is not so dramatic as those in this group.

And don't write about problems that you created for yourself. White-collar wheedling, such as padding an expense account, stealing office supplies, and even trading stocks on inside information should not be dilemmas for you. But whether you should report a coworker's misconduct is sometimes a very tough decision.

The most effective ethical essays involve a specific situation that sheds light on the difficult moral choices we all face from time to time. While you don't always have to present The Answer to a big problem, you do need to show the admissions officer how you think about and handle ethical dilemmas.

I experienced an ethical dilemma in conjunction with a litigation consulting assignment. [My company] was engaged by a national law firm to design and perform a study measuring the effects of divestiture on working capital for [two corporations]. In short, $289 million was in dispute, and the findings of our study would help resolve the case before the arbitration panel.

For seventeen months, [the consultants] worked to deliver preliminary conclusions. To support the preliminary findings, and thus finalize the engagement, I was assigned to the project and delegated responsibility for the payroll section, one of twelve subject areas under consideration. I had three months to perform a limited review, to analyze the computer payroll system, to summarize the findings, and to prepare a conclusion to be presented before the arbitrators.

Seven weeks into the project, I uncovered a flaw in a payroll methodology which wrongfully benefited [one corporation] by $.7 million. I immediately conveyed this error to the project manager, but he was unreceptive to any change. Correcting the methodology would impact other subject areas, thus requiring an additional 200 hours of fieldwork. Furthermore, he reasoned the net error was immaterial in relation to the total in question, and any major methodological change occurring in these later stages would cast doubt on the preliminary findings. Dissatisfied with the disposition, I brought the matter to the attention of the project senior manager. I agreed completely that the error was small. Nonetheless, it was a mistake. To jeopardize the reputation of [the company] seemed irrational. To emphasize my position on the matter, I stated I could not provide expert testimony unless a change in methodology transpired. Fortunately, the senior manager accepted my reasoning, and my recommendations for change were adopted.

A few months ago I was faced with a situation on my job that proved to be quite an ethical dilemma. The company I work for is a major government contractor that handles several contracts at once. The government assigns a certain amount of money to be spent on each project handled by the company. All labor and materials used to complete the project are charged to the pre-assigned allocated contract accounts. A specific set of contract numbers is used when materials and labor are consumed. These contract numbers are used for accounting purposes, as the government mandates that all materials and labor consumed be itemized by the contract to which they apply. The government explicitly prohibits using specific contract numbers on other projects than those that have already been assigned by contract agreement. If a project needs more funding, the company must renegotiate their contract with the government and not take money from programs that have adequate funds.

One of my projects ran into some difficulties, and as a result the projected production schedule deadlines became in jeopardy. To speed up the production would require more labor and materials, and consequently, more money. A problem resulted because there was simply not enough money available to fulfill the contractual obligations in a timely fashion. Due to the deadline pressure, my immediate supervisor instructed me to assign all my labor, material procurements, rework orders and rekits of assemblies to contracts that were not related to the work I was performing on. I informed him that the proper procedure was to simply request more government funding for the project through the Program Management Office.

I had recently read where General Dynamics was found guilty of similar practices that my boss was strongly advising me to perform. When I told him that I believed that taking such action was improper, he told me that this situation would last for only a short period of time. My immediate reaction was displeasure. I knew he was asking me to perform a duty that was unethical, not to mention illegal. An additional problem was that my supervisor and I had become very good friends. Despite our friendship, I felt he was unethically using his responsibilities, and to ask me to aid him confronted my personal integrity. He told me to try to understand the problems we were encountering in order to meet contract dates. With time, we could receive additional funding to complete the contract. In the mean time, in order to keep the production moving, he wanted to use other program's accounts to continue production on our contract.

After giving the situation considerable thought, I brought the matter to the attention of our manager, who consequently relieved my supervisor of his duties.

There were several reasons that prompted me to report my supervisor. First, his proposed actions were illegal. I was positive my supervisor was aware of the consequences of his actions and the incredible dilemma he was putting me in. The entire company was cognizant of the General Dynamics case and its effect. I could have been fired, or the company could have been subjected to severe penalties. I take my responsibilities as an employee seriously. I enjoy the feeling of being part of a productive team, working together to achieve a common goal. The action contemplated by my supervisor was disruptive of this team concept, and would no doubt result in counterproductive activity.

Secondly, if I complied with my supervisor's request, I would never know if he would have asked me to perform another unethical or illegal task. I value my personal integrity and moral obligations more than friendship.

This experience taught me the importance of moral integrity and teamwork. In order to have any successful enterprise you need a group of workers that possess high standards. If you do not have this integrity, there will be indecisiveness among workers, with some workers benefiting from their dishonesty and others feeling resentment over dishonest co-workers' gain. Only by having a common goal and common means of achieving that goal can an enterprise hope for success. My supervisor did not share the goals and moral responsibilities of the company. His actions were potentially disruptive and destructive. Being committed to both integrity and success, I was left with no other option but to report him.

Picture me as a child. One night as I watch my mother volunteer for the Red Cross, she receives a call from a lost woman looking for directions to a hospital. With disgust, the woman scolds, "I'm over here in [racial slur] town!" My mom, having good reason to lash out and punish the woman by giving her false information, maintains her composure and politely directs the woman to the desired location. In doing so, she teaches me a memorable lesson of self-control, tactfulness, and being true to one's values. I adopt these qualities for myself.

As an adult I continue to learn from challenging experiences that test me and force me to grow beyond my comfort zone. These experiences also shape me into the person I am today, equipping me with character qualities that I bring into the MBA environment.

Now walk with me and watch what happens when I interpret all day in Guatemala, providing medical treatment for impoverished communities. A new spirit of confidence springs forth as I stretch to learn medical terminology and decipher Mayan dialect. Amidst my fatigue and frustration, I maintain a patient manner of speaking to a young girl suffering from psychosis, comfort a grandmother writhing in arthritic pain, quell an agitated crowd, and arrange corrective surgery for a child with a club foot.

Successfully handling these situations strengthens my ability to function under pressure. Of course there is always room for the unusual when a nurse bursts into the room saying, "Keith, go to the gynecologist," causing me to spend two blushful hours scrambling for Spanish words while carefully helping her explain personal processes that I know nothing about. Talk about being taken by surprise! In the end, however, the real surprise is that I am not helping the Guatemalans nearly as much as they are helping me. They are poor yet extremely generous, sick yet optimistic and thankful. I appreciate their model of friendship and hope.

Having learned from these experiences with family and mission trips, I now carry in my business school backpack a passion for service, a willingness to experiment with new situations, and the ability to get along with diverse groups of people. Contributing these qualities allows me to succeed in the B-school environment.

Finally, in a much lighter frame of mind, I cannot help but mention that although quiet-natured, I am very personable and absolutely capable of enjoying the social aspects of life with my classmates. See, we Southerners naturally emit a special genteel charm, creating feelings of mutual comfort and contributing to the cohesiveness of a community. My classmates love it. Besides, y'all, a bit of Texas twang and Southern hospitality never hurt anybody.

ESSAYS ABOUT WORK EXPERIENCES

Business schools prefer students with some work experience. Nothing speaks louder in business than past business success. A few good years on Wall Street or in a factory can sometimes supplant a lifetime of mediocre grades.

How quickly did you learn on the job? How did you develop your skills? Did you take initiative or did you watch the clock from nine to five? Did you gain insights into the big picture of your industry, or did you simply become a master of your little routine?

Work experience can mean a lot of things besides pushing paper at the office, and we found admissions officers yearning for a wider range of topics and perspectives. A question about your past jobs is more likely to be on the application than any other, and this section includes a variety of experiences. Reporters, politicians, retail consultants, college admissions officers, and PTA presidents can display skills that are vital to other professions. And unconventional jobs and experiences are often more vivid and interesting to read about than the standard two-year stint at a bank.

Don't believe the common myth that the Ivy Leaguers who get into the plum training courses on Wall Street have an edge. You don't have to toil for Morgan Stanley to know about serious work. Harvard Business School even stated once that investment banking was at the bottom of their "desired experience" list.

All of the essays in this group tell a good story. Each has an introduction, conflict, and a resolution, and each reveals something about the writer's personality and attitude. Business schools don't want your résumé or "A Day in the Life of a 25-Year-Old Consultant." They already know that stuff. Instead, they want to know what *you* brought to a job that made you different, interesting, and more effective. Yes, you may have had the endurance to make all A's at Prestigious U., but are you creative and open-minded, too?

L ate last year, an election in [my town] led to a major disruption in my standard modus operandi on the Council. Prior to the election, I had served the role of an unofficial majority leader in a rather philosophically-divided Council. In the split of liberals vs. left-of-liberals, I led the liberal faction.

However, last November, after being unable to find a strong candidate for the vacant seat on our five-member city council, I found myself suddenly in the minority. Depression gripped me for a couple of weeks; after all, I had so many plans for our still new city, and now they all appeared dashed. Furthermore, I had previously been offered the mayorship by my colleagues on three occasions, and now when I was finally prepared to take it in anticipation of my re-election, I no longer had the guaranteed votes with which to do it.

Not being a quitter, I couldn't throw the towel in, so I sat back and developed a strategy. Although able to command only two votes on many issues of significant importance that were coming up on the Council agenda, I began to find new ways to accomplish my goals. I have learned to bring new forces to bear on issues, including organizing the community behind my position, depoliticizing previously controversial issues, and generally breaking my colleagues' voting block. This has not been easy and requires a large time investment. However, by playing off their differences and each one's desire to be the leader, I have had some successes.

The key I find is to not act like I am part of a minority. By approaching an issue from an appearance of strength, and with a superior command of the issues being debated, I am frequently able to protect my interests and accomplish what I promised my constituents. And on those occasions where I know the battle is lost, I spend extensive amounts of time with city staff assuring that even though I am going to lose I have excluded the worst possible scenarios.

Although I may not always be on the winning side of an issue now, I have succeeded in containing the damage wrought by the shift in council majorities. Beyond this, I have also been successful in publicly securing the unanimous commitment of my colleagues to elect me to the post of Mayor this spring, as well as receiving the public endorsements of both major political organizations in [my town] for my election next year.

My investment bank's internal system for the allocation of revenues and expenses among divisions produces a competitive, uncooperative relationship between investment banking and sales and trading that has resulted in the loss of business and market share for the firm. Currently, the expense for developing a product is allocated to the division making the expenditure. Revenues are allocated equally between the Investment Banking Division and a sales and trading division (i.e., Equity or Fixed Income Divisions), if employees from both divisions are involved in the transaction. An employee is then allocated revenues from his division. Since the year-end bonus, which comprises the largest portion of yearly compensation, is determined principally on an individual's net revenue, the internal accounting system sets the guidelines for working relationships within the firm.

The results of the accounting system are a stifled product development effort and poor information flow between divisions. After expensing the development of a product, a group greedily hoards its new possession to assure that somebody else does not reap the fruits of its labor without remunerating the originator of the product. Frequently, therefore, product development efforts are duplicated. Similarly, as an example, if a bond salesman has been working for weeks to develop an attractive business opportunity with a client, he often does not inform his investment banking counterpart of the prospect for fear of having to split the revenue evenly, although the investment banker may be able to assist in closing the deal through connections at the company. Meanwhile, the client receives disjointed and incomplete service despite our claim to be a "full-service" investment bank.

My solution is simple, although administratively more time-consuming. Allocate 100 percent of the revenue to each division involved, and at the year-end compensation review delve past the quantity of the revenue to determine the quality of the individual's contribution. For product development, allocate expenses to a general corporate account if the product is deemed worthy. Such a qualitative system for internal accounting imposes the burden of considering individual cases. However, within an industry bred on innovative products and integrated services, stagnation due to internal competition will result in long-term detrimental effects.

My Harvard experience was shaped by my work at Phillips Brooks House (PBH), Harvard's volunteer community service/action coordinating center (see resume). The community exposure that PBH afforded me brought to life the material in my courses. PBH provided me with a sense of purpose and the opportunity to help, both of which I felt a need to fulfill. While at PBH I realized that I enjoyed running a large organization and that my strengths lay in working with and organizing people.

After college I received a Rockefeller Fellowship which allowed me to spend nine months traveling through Asia, followed by six months of development work in Sri Lanka (see resume). Throughout my travels I was fascinated by the economic and social development of the societies I visited. In particular I found my attention was drawn to organizations either spurring, or being driven by, this development.

My observations kept returning to one common thread: no matter how original the concept, no matter how good the plan, no matter how plentiful the resources, the success of an organization was dependent upon how well it was run. What looked good on paper so often fell short due to lack of control, leadership, or efficiency. Conversely, organizations that were managed effectively often achieved what seemed impossible on paper.

My work in Sri Lanka further crystallized this point. I lived in a small village in the Hill Country where I participated in the writing of a proposal aimed at generating jobs and income for this deprived region. My research and observations made clear the desperate dearth of managers. Coops, cottage industries, development projects, loan funds, and government programs were crippled by inefficiency, disorganization, and bureaucracy. Sisira Nawaratne, the man with whom I wrote the proposal, has dedicated his life to addressing this problem and, in so doing, has provided a role model for me. His ability to turn these organizations around demonstrated that a creative manager has the potential to make the contributions to others that I hope to make during my lifetime.

The last part of my stay in Sri Lanka provided me with a very disturbing example of the importance of good management. A terrible life shattering riot broke out between the Sinhalese and the Tamils, the two main ethnic groups in the country. The Tamils were maimed, tortured, burned out. What lives they had left could only continue within the confines of a refugee camp. Fifteen camps had sprung up for the 90,000 homeless Tamils in the country's capital city, Colombo. Development workers were asked by the government to help run the camps. I volunteered along with four friends to run one of the camps, a small missionary school for 500 day students, now inundated with 4,000 homeless refugees.

The memory of my first sight of the camp will haunt me forever. People were everywhere, huddled in groups, some silently sobbing, some shrieking out their agony, others just staring off into space, contemplating the void their lives had become. The temperature hovered close to 100 degrees. Many of the refugees had not eaten or bathed for two days and were coated with the dust in which they had been sleeping. There were long lines and fights for the very limited food and two working water spigots. Flies were everywhere. The whole area was walled in and guards stood nervously outside keeping watch for the mobs that roamed the city.

After organizing the camp structurally, we tried to meet the basic physical and emotional needs of its population. Over the next five days I found myself being psychologist, chef, nurse, plumber, arbitrator, entertainer, and all too often, dictator. One moment I was unclogging a toilet with my hands, the next trying to explain to someone why his life, as he had known it, had just ended. I felt elation as we created the camp's first shower by running a hose from a neighbor's house, followed by fear as we called in the guards to break up a food fight.

During my time in the camp I gained a tremendous insight into myself. I am as proud of my contributions during that time as I am of anything I have ever done. Working together to turn that camp from a nightmare into a functioning, albeit sad and woefully inadequate, environment was the most challenging endeavor in which I have been involved. The satisfaction I derived from my contributions to that effort helped to ease the horror of the situation. Even under those circumstances I found fulfillment in organizing chaos and making things work.

When I returned to the United States I took a job campaigning for [a Senator] in his United States Senate race. I ended up running the campaign headquarters, managing the full-time volunteers, setting up the computer operation and coordinating the election day activities. These tasks offered me the chance to use my creativity, leadership skills and organizational ability. I enjoyed working closely with a large group of people to achieve a finite goal with a strict deadline and limited resources.

The campaign was my first real introduction to politics. While I learned a lot about electoral politics, I realized I wanted to learn more broadly about government. A CORO Fellowship seemed the best way to do that. A CORO Fellowship is a nine-month leadership training program in which twelve people rotate through a series of internships in government, business, labor, community and political organizations (see resume). As I moved through the internships I saw the connections, interdependence, and complexity of these organizations. I learned how almost any decision made by those in charge is influenced by the interaction between sectors. I not only became aware of the importance of good managers, I realized that many of the skills that made for a good manager in the public sector were the same as the skills vital to success in the private sector. Over and over again we interviewed leaders who had moved between jobs in business, government, politics, and non-profits. Consistently, they stressed the commonality of skills required to be successful in various fields.

My current job as [an assistant in the mayor's administration] has given me the best exposure imaginable to the consequences of good and bad management. One of our main responsibilities is to be the Mayor's eyes and ears at the Metropolitan Transportation Authority (MTA). This Authority, which has the responsibility for running the world's largest transportation system, suffers from a legacy of mismanagement which includes misallocation of resources, improper accounting, and indefinitely deferred maintenance. Supervision and accountability were lacking or non-existent. Its history provides a textbook example of how not to run an organization.

The managers currently running the MTA are charged with trying to reverse this history of neglect as quickly as possible, using severely limited resources. The management reforms they have introduced and their triage approach to efficiently stabilizing the system are slowly starting to show dividends. A political environment, however, demands quick results. Watching these officials attempting to run the MTA like a business, while at the same time balancing political pressures, has been a tremendous learning experience.

This job also has shown me how much more I need to learn about the technical skills of management before I will be prepared to help effectively run a large organization. This is the appropriate time to seek out that training, and I am convinced that [your school], for the reasons outlined in the following essay, is the best school for me.

My immediate post-MBA career goals center around my desire to eventually open a small consulting firm specializing in Change Management, Communications and Instructional Design (Training and Development). My education and career to date have helped me to shape these goals, and an MBA degree from the Cox School of Business will be a primary component in helping me to achieve these goals.

Guiding my clients through change has been an important theme in the path of my career. My clients have ranged from CEOs of Fortune 500 companies and professional athletes to county commissioners and 17-year-old high school juniors. My interaction with these clients has taken me from the cornfields of western Nebraska and the Smoky Mountains of Tennessee to the remotest islands of the Philippines and the Lapland flatlands of Sweden, near the Arctic Circle. In the course of working with these assorted clients and their varying cultures, I have found that change is the one central recurring theme that must always be addressed. Change is the constant in not only life, but also in the world of business. It is how that change is addressed that can determine the path to either success or failure.

While working as the assistant director of admissions at Southern Methodist University, I found that, to sell the University to prospective students and their parents, it was essential to create an environment that was conducive to change. Students wanted to feel comfortable in their new surroundings. Parents wanted to be reassured that their sons and daughters would be taken care of in their new environments. My goal was to remove as much uncertainty as possible about Southern Methodist University through active and continued communication throughout the college admissions process. I am proud of the fact that when I left SMU, it had reached its highest enrollment of the preceding 22 years, and that the five states with the highest yields in the incoming first-year class were all states which I was directly responsible for recruiting.

When I was charged with assisting the county auditors and treasurers offices in a transition of technology that would help bring the county infrastructure out of the 1950s, once again, it was active and effective communication that led the way to the first technology implementation in the history of county that would go live one month ahead of schedule. The look in the eyes of the 54-year-old county road and bridge superintendent, who had never used a computer to do his job, was very similar to the look in the eyes of the 17-year-old high school junior from Grand Island, Nebraska, who had never envisioned transitioning from the safety of his childhood hometown to the uncertainty of Texas.

This past year, I once again saw the same look of fear in the eyes of a 47-year-old partner, as I attempted to explain our new approach to managing the relationships of our business consulting clients. This new methodology, which would fundamentally change the way in which we approach our clients, was the most extensive change to be implemented within the firm in the history of its existence. Never before had the firm attempted to initiate a global training roll-out of such magnitude. It was the fact that we took the time and the effort to make the partners and managers comfortable with the new approach to business that contributed to the success of the project.

It is my goal to open a consulting firm that specializes in Change

Management, Communications and Instructional Design. I am confident that the skills that I would develop at the Cox School's MBA program will help to prepare me for the challenges that await, as I set forth to achieve these goals.

After four years of work experience, I realize that the people-oriented and planning aspects of business interest me. In light of this discovery, my career goal is to become an expert at strategic planning. I want to support this ability by understanding how to identify, develop, and deploy the best people to implement the strategies. My professional experience has prepared me with a foundation on which to build toward this goal.

"JC Penney—I love your style." Thus sang our popular ad. As an Inventory Analyst for this stylish company, I forecasted catalog and Internet demand for men's apparel. Challenged by a project aimed at reducing the return rate for men's shirts, I contributed my analyses to interdepartmental planning efforts among the buying, advertising, and brand management areas. My efforts helped the team re-design the fit of the shirts and yielded high-impact visual presentations that allowed the customer to see the merchandise better. Reducing the return rate saved the company $1,000,000 over a six-month period. After earning two workload increases, I moved to the sporting goods area. Focusing my attention on surplus reduction, I successfully coached my suppliers through new inventory procurement procedures that increased inventory turnover and reduced lost sales on high-dollar merchandise.

While at JC Penney I also used my relational skills to assist with college recruitment efforts by interviewing candidates and conducting career fairs. In the process, I creatively presented two workshops that won high ratings from students at a national conference in Austin. Eventually, I looked for new challenges and desired to expand my skill set. Switching to the insurance industry offered me that opportunity.

As a Chubb underwriter, I have identified and begun pursuing $40,000 in potential business with companies facing property, machinery breakdown, and transportation risks. I set prices, write customized insurance packages, and grow my accounts through a network of independent agents. While this knowledge is invaluable, I have yet to truly discover my professional niche.

However, when I examine the appealing qualities of my jobs, the people-oriented and the planning aspects of business interest me. That is why I define my career goal around strategic planning. An MBA program having a powerful general management orientation and offering the practicality of hands-on training is the best vehicle for me to prepare for this career change. Studying how various business functions operate and complement each other gives me a broad, multi-faceted understanding of key issues. Practical activities such as consulting projects and overseas study trips allow me to explore different fields of interest and apply classroom concepts while gaining worthwhile problem solving experience. The experience also sharpens my ability to productively negotiate, persuade, motivate, and resolve conflict with people regardless of our unique personalities. Upon completing my MBA, I will be capable of creating new business opportunities and able to lead companies in developing the human talent that they need.

I recently read Robert Dedman's book, *The King of Clubs*, where he stresses that to achieve success, one must, "Plan [his] work and work [his] plan." After reading the book, I realized that my greatest successes have resulted from following his paradigm by setting a goal based on my priorities and working hard to achieve that goal. Throughout my educational and professional career, I have found that when my goals and priorities were clear, working hard was easy because I was motivated.

During my last two years in college, I worked at a country club in the tennis retail store. The position was one of the most enlightening experiences of my life. Unlike most clubs, the tennis store manager was an independent contractor who rented the retail space from the club. As a result, the store was a stand-alone business, and the manager had full control of the tennis program and the store's operations. He was an outstanding businessman and had all the qualities of an entrepreneur. My interview was conducted in a trailer, since the new tennis complex was still under construction. Upon moving into the new facility, I showed the most interest in installing the computer software, thus I was given full control over the transition to the computers. I learned the inventory, sales, and scheduling programs, and set up member databases. Within a few months, the store was more efficient and I was training the staff on its usage. I was also given full responsibility to manage the men's tennis league. By increasing my responsibilities, I began to learn the keys to running a small business. The manager taught me to how to strike a balance between increasing revenues and satisfying customers without sacrificing the growth of the business.

I saw the impact of the changes in technology in my position at the country club, which led me to realize that I was very interested in technology. As a psychology major, I had studied the impact of human thought at many levels, but it did not seem to apply to everyday life. Moreover, as a senior, it was too late to pursue a business degree, but I discovered the business foundations certification program for non-business majors and enrolled. I loved the business classes and decided to continue a concentrated business education through a graduate business program in a few years. Equipped with a solid goal, I began working toward a job offer in the technology industry. After learning how difficult it is to participate in business recruiting as a liberal arts major, I sent my resume directly to technology companies and was offered a position as a Business Analyst at Electronic Data Systems (EDS) in Plano, Texas.

I began working in the Decision Support group, which performs competitive analysis. By comparing the operating costs of EDS to those of our competitors with similar workloads and size, I derive a reasonable expense level for operations. My analyses also uncover areas where the technical delivery managers need to improve the efficiency of their structure. In addition, my position brings together the activities of the financial and technical organizations. Innovative solutions are researched every day in the new economy. At EDS, talented people perform this research, but the people performing the research have different loyalties. The financial organization at EDS views the company's funds and sets financial budgets, but has a very limited view of how improvements in technology and new services help EDS deliver superior solutions to clients. The technical delivery organization ensures that reliable services are delivered to the clients, but is often unaware of the financial goals of the corporation. The inconsistency between these two groups often prevents positive change for EDS, while at the same time I look outside EDS and see that the thriving IT industry demands continuous improvement in order to survive. I consistently struggle with the inability of EDS to evaluate and implement new technologies. A Cox MBA will prepare me to analyze and manage the innovation that has come with the new economy.

Upon graduating with an MBA, I plan to manage a strategic planning organization in an IT form. I will satisfy a specific niche between the operational and financial arms of my future employer. My accomplishments and professional success over the last two years have given me a strong foundation in business. However, I realize that to succeed in the new economy, I need to complete an MBA that concentrates on strengthening my skills in managing technology, innovation, globalization, and entrepreneurial opportunity.

Having completed one semester of the Professional MBA Program at Cox, I have seen the opportunities that Cox offers its students. Because of my work schedule, I was unable to take advantage of many of these opportunities. I value the "Cox Advantage," and I want to be able to fully optimize the resources at Cox. To accomplish this, I feel that I need to be able to concentrate on my study of business without the added time pressures of a full-time job. I know what I need to do, I have set my goal, and I will work hard to achieve my goal. I hope that you are able to afford me the opportunity to "plan my work and work my plan."

The emergence and rapid growth of the internet has had and will continue to have a profound impact on business culture. The use of the internet offers people and businesses not just more opportunity, but opportunities that are different in kind and require new types of strategy and ways of thinking. Fully taking advantage of these opportunities calls for individuals who are versed in the application of the developing technology and who understand that each unique business requires its own unique approach.

Through my work at CitySearch.com, I have had the opportunity to observe the impact of this new technology on long-established businesses. Not only have I introduced many of these businesses to the possibilities that exist on the internet for the first time, but I have also crafted new solutions for their marketing needs. Working on the cutting edge of this industry has opened my eyes and, in turn, my customers' eyes to all of the possibilities that exist within the internet.

A few instances will suffice to demonstrate the tangible benefits that companies can derive from fully utilizing their internet resources. Company X was able to triple its response rate when I installed an interactive form on their web site. Company Y enhanced its positioning on search engines after I restructured the home page, focusing on key words and page names. Company Z was able to streamline its once labor-intensive gift certificate procedure when I created an on-line functionality that allowed the user to go directly to the web site, purchase the gift certificate, personalize it, and send it directly to the recipient.

All of these businesses were beneficiaries of a movement that enhances the flow of information. This transition is arguably more dramatic than any that business has undergone in at least five hundred years. Businesses cater to customers whom they might never have otherwise reached. Communication between businesses is now faster, easier, cheaper, and more efficient than ever before. The very concept of the marketplace as a physical location where buyer and seller interact may soon be obsolete. While it is impossible to envision the specific changes that might take place in the next ten years (based on improvements in the technology, the availability of that technology, etc.), it is clear that the internet is going to continue to evolve and accelerate. A business that fails to incorporate these changes in time will be left behind.

I plan to remain in the forefront of this industry. It is exciting to see the changes that the internet has brought about. I feel confident that over the next generation these changes are going to continue to impact business in ways we can't even imagine. Furthermore, as is already apparent, these developments will affect society not only in the commercial sphere, but in many other areas as well. I am eager to take part in this transformation.

ESSAYS ABOUT THE MBA

This should be the easiest essay to write. You've probably gone through all the arguments for and against business school a hundred times while deciding whether to apply. So for this essay, all you really have to do is put your thoughts on paper clearly and coherently.

You should use this type of essay to convince admissions officers—as you have already convinced yourself—that you could advance much farther in your career and contribute much more to society with an MBA. If you can provide examples of accomplishments and show that you *need* more business education for continued success, your application will be hard to ignore.

Many of the applicants in this group had reached an impasse in their careers. Some opted for business school to learn the skills they needed to tackle more innovative projects. Others, especially from journalism and advertising, saw a need in their industry to bridge the gap between the creative people and the "front office." They knew that adding business knowledge to their creative talents could make them proficient executives who would also understand their less financially minded employees.

A number of applicants felt that their lack of an MBA was limiting their future and pushing them onto unfulfilling career tracks. They wanted to acquire business skills that would augment their existing talents and reveal more rewarding opportunities. One applicant was returning to school after twelve years to enhance the work he was doing in his native India.

However, explaining how an MBA would help you is the easy part. After all, most people in business would be better off with an MBA. Your task, then, is to analyze your goals carefully and demonstrate why you should be one of the privileged few who receives top business training. Why would *you* be more valuable to society with an MBA than the other five thousand applicants?

Simply put, if you can convince an admissions officer that you will be more valuable with an MBA than the others, your essay will be successful.

There is an old Chinese saying: "The value of a sword cannot be judged when the sword stands alone in a corner; only when it is wielded by an expert can one see its true worth." That is how I think of an MBA.

I have worked with quite a few account executives who have MBAs and I find them, as a rule, more competent and rounded than their non-MBA counterparts. There are certain things that are intrinsic to possessors of graduate degrees; they are slightly older, they are intelligent enough to be accepted into degree programs, they have learned (one way or another) to deal with the work required to earn their degrees, and they've had to work closely with people not of their choosing. So in a way, MBAs are broken-in. They're used to inordinate amounts of work with people they may not necessarily like or respect, frightening deadlines and thinking so hard they almost bleed from their ears. They've been through "Basic."

However, the AEs I've worked with got hired at some pretty incredible salaries and I'm not sure all of them were worth it. Some, yes. All, no. I think the main problem was a large percentage of them had 4 years of undergrad, then 3 years of B-School *before* their first job. No Real-World experience, no Real-World judgment. And that was their Achilles' heel. They were well-versed in theory, but hell, in theory, a bumble bee can't fly.

I think many of the problems they caused could have been avoided if all MBA programs required 4 or 5 years of work experience. See how far *that* idea gets with this "gotta-be-a-millionaire-by-the-time-I'm-thirty" generation. A lot of them figure an MBA is the ticket to The Good Life. Very possibly. Corporations wine and dine B-Schoolers in their Junior year, for crissakes. Hell, I knew a Harvard kid who was a star, and these multi-nationals were falling all over each other to get on his dance card. He scored a summer internship in a finance company that paid him more for a summer than I made last year, and I ain't doing bad. They guaranteed him a job after he graduated. Go figure. And I still can't decide if the MBA made him worth that much or if he was a natural-born finance-Einstein.

Some guys take an MBA, get into a little company and make it sing. Bango. "New Faces" in Forbes. Others, well, there's the story of Harley-Davidson. It was acquired by AMF. They sent in a team of hot-shot MBAs. An MBA's job is to make money. Make a profit, then increase profits. I figure they were "Punk" MBAs (like the ones I mentioned before . . . first job right out of school, very mercenary). They probably figured that if they turned enough of a profit, AMF would promote them out of there or they would use their successes to jump to another company *before* the long-term effects of their decisions became evident. I can't testify to that; all I know is that the quality of the company's products went straight down the flusher and in three years, you couldn't give those things away. Bikers were turning to Hondas. Harleys could belch up their insides at any moment. Cheap materials and cheaper techniques. Non-existent quality control. And the new models went totally against the grain of the true Harley buyer. They even tried to market a cafe racer, which was as European as Brie, to a buyer who would only eat Apple Pie. It was total disregard for their primary market and total delusion to think they could turn a Hog into a Thoroughbred and that anyone would buy such an odd creature as other than a curiosity. I *can* testify to those results. I worked in a motorcycle shop then.

Anyway, AMF didn't put up a fight when Harley wanted to go independent. Everyone blamed the Bean Counters for the screw-ups. The Managers. Bottom-Liners. They short-termed the company to the brink of extinction.

The strengths and weaknesses of an MBA? Look not to the sword, but to the swordsman.

I want to shepherd Earth's move into Space. That is, I want to be one of the people responsible for removing the barriers preventing the productive use and exploration of Space. The knowledge and experience I have gained at Cornell, Citibank, and NASA's Johnson Space Center will help me accomplish this task. The two career goals I discuss here result from my analysis of the risks endangering the movement I want to encourage.

Many of the technical risks involved in going to and living in Space for long periods of time have been solved. For example, the American, European, Canadian, and Japanese Space Station will have a closed water system. This recycling of water will make room for other supplies on the logistics flights serving the Space Station. Solutions like the closed water systems are expensive. The aerospace industry is working hard to lower these costs.

Those technical risks that still exist do not trouble me. I have found many people at Cornell and NASA excited about producing the engineering refinements needed to make the technical risks of space travel and exploration negligible. I want to provide them the opportunities to make those advances by reducing the financial, political, and organizational risks associated with the development of space.

The prime financial risks associated with investment in Space result not from the failure of one or two projects, but from investors' inability to recognize when good investments can be made in space systems. Strategies to remedy the financial sector's inability to evaluate investments in space systems call for a gradual approach so investors can learn how to profit from space ventures. In the case of private launch systems, this gradual approach requires some project such as the development of a simple, small-scale launch system. My work at Citibank and in political economy courses at Cornell has convinced me that this system must serve a realistic need. Several companies, including Space Services Inc. of Houston, have tried unsuccessfully to market simple launch vehicles. These companies have produced launch systems without aiming their product at any particular set of customers. In an earth-bound analogy, they are providing only a truck when they must first find a customer who needs some sort of transportation.

The need to provide a service to a customer in space leads to one conclusion. For the foreseeable future, the one and only customer is the International Space Station. Research at the Johnson Space Center indicates that the logistics needs of the Space Station cannot be met by the Space Shuttle alone. Under this condition, the most likely venture to fulfill a need of this customer is one that can ensure the accurate and speedy delivery of small payloads to the Space Station. I plan to create an organization to provide this service within the first few years after I complete business school. Such a venture would require a moderate amount of capital. The key technology, safe operations in proximity to the Space Station, would be transferable to other ventures such as satellite refueling. The lessons learned in this undertaking would reduce the uncertainties for subsequent payload systems' development and thus reduce the associated financial risks.

Success in a project like this would have the same beneficial effects on general space haulage that the U.S. Postal Service's early use of airmail had on the aviation industry. In conjunction with decreased costs resulting from new technology and program experience, the success of the small payload service would make other commercial systems possible. The increased availability of spare parts on the

Space Station provided by this service would reduce the risks associated with designing and operating commercial payloads on the station.

The small payload service can only serve as part of a larger strategy to reduce the risks of going to Space. Additional actions must be taken to overcome the economic, institutional, and political risks of building an infrastructure where no industry exists and of manufacturing a product where no infrastructure exists. Work I did for several government courses I took at Cornell convinced me that societies manage risk by creating institutions. In a closely related example, NASA was born out of the National Advisory Committee for Aeronautics as part of the reaction to the risks posed by Sputnik. My plans are based upon expectations that a similar type of behavior will be repeated in dealing with the problem of space commercialization. To be specific, I want to be responsible for the division of NASA as it exists now into a research and exploration agency and a space infrastructure agency. NASA needs to be split up because its research goals conflict with its operational goals. This conflict manifests itself in many ways. Currently, flight equipment is designed so that it has many potential uses. This suits the research side of NASA. Operations philosophy, on the other hand, calls for simple, dedicated equipment that fills only a limited set of operational requirements. Simplicity and limited scope make operational equipment reliable and inexpensive.

The research and exploration agency would draw upon the parts of NASA responsible for successes like the Apollo and the Voyager programs. The infrastructure agency would have its roots in NASA's current Space Shuttle and Space Station programs. Such an operations agency would eventually be made a private company or dissolved in favor of private organizations. With the eventual split, each agency will have a distinct role and also a distinct set of problems. I want to take on the challenge of minimizing those problems by being the one responsible for the transition of NASA into those two new agencies.

The role of the research and exploration agency will be much the same as the role the space research sections of NASA had up through the Soviet-American Apollo-Soyez Test Project in 1975. Its role will also encompass the aeronautical investigations that NASA does. I recognize the possibility that this agency can easily be forgotten if it does not run programs such as a Manned Mars Mission that capture the public's imagination. Still, this possibility is not a valid argument against splitting up NASA. The level of funding for space research should be a legislative decision. If the public is persuaded that this agency is necessary, it will get the funds it needs.

To make this agency work, its organization must promote the development of clear research and exploration goals without stifling creativity and discovery. This requires excellent communications within the agency. The leaders of the research and engineering organization will need to change the way NASA manages its research organization now if they want to improve communications. I expect to learn how to manage that change while at the School of Management.

As one of the creators of the space infrastructure agency, I must find a way to build the infrastructure necessary for industry in Space to be viable. To do this, the space infrastructure agency must fulfill the role of the market in both the launch vehicle and space industry sectors. Foremost, the agency must provide the incentives and information that markets in more mature sectors generate. Comsat, in creating a domestic and international market for U.S. satellite manufacturers, has performed this role for the communications satellite industry. I understand that to recreate Comsat's success in a different sector, under different external economic conditions, will require skill, hard work, and luck. Here again, the School of Management can provide the skills I need.

I have described lofty goals here in more ways than one. I have chosen these goals because they motivate me and because I know that even if I do not attain them completely, I will still be satisfied. To get close to achieving these goals, I need to become better at making risky decisions and recovering from poor ones. My work at Cornell,

Citibank, and NASA has brought me to the point where I can identify the risks I must overcome to achieve the goals I have chosen. The knowledge and confidence I gain at business school will allow me to run a small package delivery service to orbit successfully. That experience, in turn, will prepare me to manage the creation of the two new agencies out of NASA that I see as necessary to promote Earth's move into Space.

The pattern of my life, the series of choices I have made, has been shaped by two divergent tendencies: a tendency toward idealism and a tendency toward pragmatism. At extremes, I have made clay bricks to build a primary school in rural Africa, and I have worked in the largest law firm in Boston. At times I have been frustrated by the seeming incompatibility of these two tendencies, and yet I value them both. Fortunately, I have discovered that my idealism and my pragmatism converge in a way that I find deeply satisfying in the field of arts management.

In stating that my career goal is to be an arts manager, I invite three questions: Why management? Why art? And why the two together?

Why Management? I believe that I possess certain strengths and qualities which are essential for a good manager, notably: social skills, organizational ability, resourcefulness, analytical ability, and a fund of knowledge. In both my education and my work experience I have made choices which have allowed me to utilize and develop these strengths and qualities. My desire to be a professional manager stems from the satisfaction I get from using them.

I like people, and I have developed the skills needed to work with a wide variety of personalities. When I worked at a bluegrass music festival as Assistant to the Producer, I interacted with everyone from the county fire chief to the owners of a vegetarian food stand, from dozens of eager volunteer staff members to an audience member who complained about the size and shape of his neighbor's lawn chair, and from newspaper reporters to the lead musicians—literally hundreds of people during the four days of the festival. In my current position as Director of Development at an Off-Broadway style theatre I work closely with the Board of Directors. The twenty-three directors present a variety of personalities, backgrounds and expectations that I must accommodate, while trying to advocate my own views, in our frequent meetings. These two experiences have added breadth and depth, respectively, to my social skills.

Perhaps my greatest strength is my ability to organize. Most recently, I have used this skill in producing fundraising events. The first step of course is to design an event that will appeal to potential donors and thus generate maximum income. The organizational challenge is then to solve a myriad of logistical problems including invitations, decorations, music, food and drink. I must make sure that each task is assigned to a volunteer on the events committee and that the volunteers complete their jobs on time. Ultimately I serve as the coordinator of the parts, the manager of the details.

My current job also demands that I be very resourceful. The Theatre Project Company has only nine full-time staff members to run a professional mainstage theatre and a touring children's theatre company. As a result, each staff member has a tremendous amount of responsibility and often has to wear more than one hat. Furthermore, the Theatre's chronic lack of financial resources creates numerous problems for which the staff must find quick and creative solutions. Last summer, due to an unfortunate set of circumstances, the Theatre found itself without a Business Manager. I took on this position, in addition to holding my own position, for two and a half months until a new Business Manager was hired. When I started, I knew nothing about accounting or financial management, but among other tasks I had to keep the Company's books, file the final financial report for our season with the state arts council, handle all disbursements and receivables, and do the weekly payroll. For the most part, I learned by doing. It was at once exhausting and exhilarating.

My undergraduate education at Yale helped me develop my analytical ability. As an English major, I wrote many essays. In each case I had to examine a piece of literature, extract the important bits of information (i.e. the information relevant to my essay topic), and then organize those bits of information into a coherent statement. This was particularly difficult in the case of my senior thesis. I chose to write about the work of South African playwright Athol Fugard, and at the time there were no secondary sources to aid me in my analysis. I was a critical pioneer: I read all of his plays, probing each one deeply, and tried to determine the essence of his work. Undoubtedly, the essay on Fugard represents some of the finest work I did while at Yale. I continue to use my analytical ability, the ability to separate a whole into its constituents for examination and interpretation, in less formal, less academic ways. For example, whenever I write a corporate or foundation grant proposal for the Theatre, I review the potential donor's application guidelines, determine which of our programs falls within those guidelines, and decide which aspects of the Theatre's history and activities need emphasis in the proposal.

Thus far I have limited my discussion of managerial strengths and qualities to skills. While not a skill, a fund of knowledge is essential for a good manager. By "fund of knowledge" I mean a large body of specific information, gleaned from formal education and from experience. The acquisition of knowledge always has been one of my goals. Philosophically I agree with the goals of a liberal arts education, and at Yale I took a wide variety of courses. Outside of my education also I have sought to expose myself to numerous situations and ideas, through travel, athletics and voluntarism.

Why art? It is difficult to talk about art without sounding either silly or sententious, even if sincere. I believe, however, that it is the responsibility of professionals in the arts to articulate the value of art to society.

Through their work artists offer the other members of society a new perspective, a chance to stand in someone else's shoes, even if only for a short while. In accepting their offer, we acquire knowledge, knowledge which may help us to better ourselves and our world. Art enlightens.

Furthermore, art has the rare power to create community. Art is produced for people to see or hear; it is meant to be shared. In an age when both the church and the family are disintegrating, art can still bring people and their ideas together. Art transcends differences among individuals.

For as long as I can remember I have believed that art is important. The knowledge I have gained from my literature studies at Yale, my jobs in the arts, and my participation in various cultural activities has enhanced my innate appreciation of art.

Why the two together? Management is what I'm good at; art is what I believe in. Together they provide an intellectual and emotional balance which I find personally satisfying. More importantly, I am convinced that this balance will enable me to work to my fullest and thus make the greatest possible contribution to society.

After witnessing the exciting ties between energy and finance as an investment banker in the Global Energy and Power Group at UBS Warburg, I am eager to pursue a career in strategic business development for a prominent energy company. But in order to be fully equipped with the skills, knowledge and relationships such a position will require, it is essential that I devote two years of study in a top-notch MBA program. With opportunities like the Macgregor Energy Institute, the Global Leadership Program, and the Executive Mentor Program, which are unique to Cox, I am convinced that SMU is the right education for me.

While I consider my three years as an investment banking analyst invaluable, I am eager for a professional experience on the corporate side of the energy industry. I have learned to work with great attention to detail even under tight time constraints to produce financial models and presentations that are accurate and insightful so that our clients can see clearly the recommendations we are making. I have had the benefit of meeting regularly with top-level executives and find myself quite comfortable and confident in briefing them on our work. Having developed trusting relationships with such key energy industry players, I look forward to helping my future employer—be it Halliburton, BP, TXU, or another major energy company—develop strategic partnerships within the energy community.

But my relationship-building skills and valuation know-how must be balanced with tested business ethics, advanced accounting skills, and risk management strategies. In reviewing the Cox curriculum, I know that I will emerge from MBA school well-equipped to serve as a valuable asset in helping my future employer strategically advance on sound financial ground.

As I've learned firsthand about the business practices and goals of energy companies such as Torch Offshore, W-H Energy, AES and MCN Energy, I am intrigued by the many facets of their day-to-day business. Strategic know-how is a must as they work to discern how to divide their capital appropriately between hard asset expenditures, research and development efforts, and the development of an e-business strategy. Just as other industries have capitalized on the business to business potential of the Internet, the energy industry must move in this direction for the purposes of streamlining the transport of offshore drilling rigs, for example, between buyer and seller in the most cost-effective manner. I believe a Cox MBA will equip me with the instincts and the tools to advocate innovative solutions for my post-MBA employer.

The global nature of the energy industry is integral to its identity and success. And because I am interested in working for a period of time in a foreign country for a company with worldwide operations, I am eager to make the most of Cox's Global Leadership Program. Having worked on transactions in places like Australia, Kazakhstan, Scotland, South America, and United Arab Emirates, I recognize the cultural barriers that most large companies must overcome. During my time at Warburg, we represented BP on a project in South America where I valued a pipeline that transverses both Bolivia and Brazil. Not only were there cultural differences between our bankers from North America and the clients from South America, but there were also challenging differences between the Bolivian and Brazilian counterparts—language barriers, expectations and professional customs. Although we were formally representing only the seller, we found ourselves serving as an arbitrator—trying to smooth over the relations between both parties. We successfully completed the deal, but I know that an experience such as the Global Leadership Program would sharpen and broaden my cultural perspectives and cross-border business methodologies and ethics. I look forward to the opportunity to meet with foreign executives, to observe operations, and to soak in cultural nuances.

The Cox MBA curriculum is well-suited to help me accomplish my professional goals. Through the rigorous MBA course load, the powerful networking among alumni, the relationship I will form with my Executive Mentor, and even the meetings with executives in the Global Leadership Program, I believe I will be well-equipped to serve as a valuable asset to a global energy company.

I am an electrical engineering graduate. Major courses undertaken by me included electronics and introduction to telecommunication, besides regular subjects pertaining to electrical engineering. The curriculum also included introduction to computers and computer programming.

I started my career as an engineering officer in the microwave communication stream in the Indian Air Force. My main aim behind joining the IAF was to serve my country. I also expected to learn discipline, focus and management and to be a confident professional after six years of experience as an officer. The experience in IAF exceeded my expectations. In addition to what was expected, I learned how to get things done with limited resources/support while meeting deadlines. The training and experience in microwave communications taught me the use and importance of computing and communications to organizations and managers.

A large part of my experience in IAF was in the area of planning and implementation of new communication projects. I wanted to use and broaden this experience and was looking for a suitable opportunity to do the same on completion of my tenure in IAF. Small Industries Development Bank of India (SIDBI), a development finance institution engaged mainly in providing long-term finance (direct as well as through other intermediaries) for implementing projects offered such an opportunity. I therefore joined SIDBI. SIDBI is the premier institution for promotion, development and finance of small-scale industries in India. It had annual loan sanctions of over USD 2500 million and disbursements of over USD 1500 million. It has a developmental focus and extends assistance mainly to projects relevant to needs of small, tiny and micro enterprises. SIDBI is among the top 50 development finance institutions of the world in terms of assets/annual sanctions according to the Banker magazine of London.

Having served in SIDBI for six years, and after total work experience of 12 years, I now want to further enlarge and enrich my work. I feel I should draw on my experience so far and also on my strengths as a person to do so meaningfully. My strengths are intelligence, ability to evaluate ideas, think things through and total commitment to whatever I apply myself to. I therefore want to work at middle/senior management level in the area of project planning and implementation in a large corporation involved in telecommunications or a related field like internet service/infrastructure. An MBA should prepare me for and provide an opportunity to work in such an organization.

I therefore want to enroll for an MBA with finance and information technology as major subject areas. The graduate school will teach me all the concepts and tools necessary for my work. It will also provide an opportunity to interact with highly talented fellow students and teachers. This will serve to broaden my horizons, provide innumerable learning opportunities and also provide opportunities to occasionally contribute to the learning of other students.

Large companies working in the area of communication tend to have global operations. An MBA from your school, with its diverse faculty and students from many countries, will be particularly suitable for such a career. An MBA from your school, which is situated in Dallas, home to many companies involved in communication, will be ideal for fulfilling my post-MBA career objective.

ESSAYS ABOUT ACCOMPLISHMENTS

Some of the accomplishments in this group of essays are extraordinary. One applicant helped raise $2 million through a direct-mail campaign, while another founded a novel nonprofit corporation that was praised by national media. A third person started a small airline—while he was still in college!

Most likely, you haven't done anything quite so spectacular, but don't let that discourage you. If you're not sure which of your accomplishments you're most proud of, read through this chapter with an eye for the similarities among these applicants. Each one was confronted with a difficult problem and solved it with creativity. They were confident and innovative enough to improvise when unique situations arose. And they succeeded. It's that quality—the bold, entrepreneurial spirit—that many admissions officers told us they admire.

When you're choosing your finest accomplishment, try to look for an instance when you solved a tough problem with an unconventional insight, or took an entrepreneurial path around the bureaucracy to get something done. Quality, not quantity, is important. Notice that these essays vary widely in length, yet they all represent successful applicants. Short essays are risky; be sure you have made a descriptive statement. On the other hand, don't write so many words that your reader gets bored, distracted, or sleepy.

Remember, the actual accomplishment is usually unimportant to the admissions officers. What they really want to see is how you *think* about a task—and how effectively you can communicate your thoughts in an essay.

I began my career as a scientist, but I am now director of a corporation I founded and developed. Several years ago, I began planning a national gene bank of the rarest American plant types. *Time* called the organization I started and now direct "an unprecedented program, by far the most comprehensive to date." *Science*, *The New York Times*, *Washington Post*, and Associated Press network, among others, have all featured major stories about it.

I have learned that I can set ambitious goals for an organization, attract financial support, build an effective staff, and most importantly, produce results. It is far more satisfying than the technical work I did previously, and convinces me that my career will continue in business administration. At the same time, I do not consider myself an excellent manager; I often improvise when I should be able to rely on practiced skills and an informed sense of perspective. I need formal training to sharpen the entrepreneurial and managerial skills I have developed.

I particularly want to attend your school because of its unsurpassed reputation for training general business managers able to function in environments that demand scientific and quantitative abilities. The integration of business training with my knowledge of the basic sciences would give me powerful skills for work in the high technology industries. Biotechnology, in particular, is only now becoming a true economic activity. I am convinced that there are many unrealized opportunities to develop simple, extremely useful applications of existing biotechnologies, such as screening plants used in non-western medicine for active pharmaceuticals. No U.S. drug company is now investigating such plants, although a quarter of all present prescription medicines are plant derivatives. Nonetheless, I view my past training as a possible asset to my career, not a constraint; I would expect study at your school to broaden my perspective on possible careers, as well as providing substantive information.

My commitment to a career in management has developed slowly. When I was an undergraduate, I was the student founder and resident director of Shaw House, the "residential college" for the Boston College Honor's program. I organized a program intended to be an intellectual and cultural focus for the House, the Program as a whole, and the entire residential campus. Later, while I was in graduate school, I was one of two leaders of research expeditions with about twenty participants. These trips have taken me to uninhabited islands and coastal jungles in the Caribbean, Central America and Africa. Leading the expeditions demonstrated to me that I could build an effective, task-oriented group. But at the time, I saw both of these activities as secondary to my studies in basic biology and resource management.

Within a few years after graduate school, I began planning the Center for Plant Conservation, now the national gene bank for rare American plant types. I designed the Center as a nonprofit corporation, but one focussed on measurable accomplishment. It is rapidly building a permanent genetic reserve of over 3,000 plant types, almost all of which were previously inaccessible and likely to be lost entirely.

The Center combines twenty-five of the most notable scientific institutions in the United States—including Harvard, the Smithsonian and the Department of Agriculture—in a program well beyond the capacity of any preexisting organization. While the Center was the first program of its kind, several countries, including mainland China, are considering it as a model for plant genetic reserves of their own. The Canadian Centre for Plant Conservation is already operating.

I conceived of the Center five years ago. Today it is a major not-for-profit corporation with a structure analogous to a commercial franchising chain. More than sixty scientists and technicians at institutions throughout the country are building collections of living plants, seeds and tissue cultures as part of the Center's program, and a staff of seven, including three with Ph.D.s, a J.D. and an M.B.A., coordinates its operations at the national level.

Building the Center has refined all my basic abilities, strengthening some and tempering others. More than any other experience, it has helped me develop both the external abilities and internal qualities of leadership—and there is little of my experience that is not required of me as a leader of a rapidly growing organization.

While I was still in school I saw my organizational roles as secondary to my scientific training. I am now convinced that my technical education is background for a career in management.

As a second-year Analyst in BT Real Estate, I was a member of a four-person team, acting as exclusive financial advisor to Radnor Corporation ("Radnor") in connection with the sale of three Southwestern shopping centers: Temecula Town Center, Lemon Grove Plaza, and Greenway Park Plaza. My division had a strong, ten-year relationship with Radnor, having sold over $800 million of assets for them. Soon after the due diligence process began, we realized these properties were not well-managed. Leases were missing; capital expenses could not be accounted for; and little effort was being made to lease vacant space. Frustration, tempers and patience were many times near explosive levels. As the most junior team member, exposed to multiple elements of the deal, I saw an opportunity to alleviate the tension.

Having worked with Radnor extensively before, I knew most of the players and personalities. I recommended a plan to my BT team whereby I would split my time as needed in order to be on site at the three properties, taking charge of knowing everything about the tenant leases. Having one person in charge would increase efficiency and keep the deal organized and on track. I also volunteered to design the Offering Memorandum, working with the design artist and local photographers in capturing the functionality of these properties.

As my BT Real Estate responsibilities evolved, I found myself playing a different role on three teams: (1) On site, I led the lease review and underwriting process with eight local Radnor employees. My role here facilitated a smooth, uniform and consistent lease review process, enhanced morale, and generated a well-polished finished product for potential investors to review. (2) With my BT Real Estate counterparts in New York, I coordinated my on-site team results. This kept the deal's momentum moving forward by providing accurate, efficient information on a daily basis; it also alleviated pressure for my manager and counterparts. (3) I served as a liaison between Radnor's executive management team in Philadelphia and Radnor's own employees on- and off-site. This provided an accurate, timely and direct dissemination of information to the top, and fortified the headway Radnor's on- and off-site employees were making. As a result of these roles, my BT Real Estate team could focus on the deal and its profitability for all parties involved. I was instrumental in keeping communication lines open, information flowing, and morale alive.

This accomplishment points to my "multi-task" leadership abilities—providing expertise; being a resource; setting momentum; supplying inspiration; resolving conflict; and finding alternate routes. It also points to my "multi-level" team management abilities—differing ages and experience. Finally, it points to my ability to achieve the vision that was set. In the end, BT Real Estate reached its objective, achieving record sales figures ($65 million in total) for three shopping centers in the Southwestern United States. I am glad to have played a major role in achieving that result.

My involvement with Collegiate Air Service as President and Founder and my work overseeing the leasing program for Biltmore Place in downtown Los Angeles both illustrate my project management and leadership abilities. While my positions with Collegiate Air Service and with Biltmore Place were very different, both required an able project manager and leadership in order to succeed. In each instance, I managed the process of bringing human and capital resources together to fulfill a need. My involvement was instrumental in realizing certain objectives and in maximizing value.

While my activity with the flying service occurred more than three years ago, it is a significant achievement that illustrates my entrepreneurial and managerial skills from an early age. Early in my senior year of college, I was frustrated with my difficulty in building the airtime required for advanced pilot ratings. The cost of flying a two-seat, single-engine plane was prohibitive, not to mention the significantly larger cost of twin-engine aircraft. My objective was to log flight time at a relatively low cost in as large and complex an aircraft as possible. My idea was to provide the University community with an airtaxi service. This would fulfill my objectives and provide customers with a low-cost means of transportation. I consulted an aviation attorney, insurance agents, and a local fixed base operator (a plane leasing company) to determine the feasibility of setting up such a service. At first, there were questions regarding compliance with FAA regulations, liability, and licensing, which were all quickly solved. I set up the service as a nonprofit organization to avoid the arduous and expensive licensing process. Overhead for the venture was extremely low because my only expenses were the attorney's fees, insurance costs, and limited marketing materials explaining the service. A fleet of planes with four to nine seats were put at my disposal. My only obligation to the fixed base operator was payment for the actual time the aircraft was used. I contacted other students who were qualified pilots and explained to them the idea and the opportunities it offered them. Three other pilots agreed to fly for the service. I instituted certain policies and procedures for running the operation, which included performance standards, weather minimums, schedules for pilot availability, and billing procedures. It was a thrilling experience to create a small nonprofit airtaxi operation from what was originally an idea to maximize my airtime. During the year, we logged approximately 60 hours of flight time worth over $4,500.

A more recent example of my leadership abilities and managerial potential is my work as a member of the on-site development team overseeing the renovation and construction of the Biltmore Hotel and complex (Biltmore Place)—a mixed-use project comprised of 410,000 square feet of office space, 707 hotel rooms, 30,000 square feet of retail space, and a 368-stall above-ground garage. One of my major duties was to oversee the in-house leasing staff. Acting as the owner's representative, I organized and managed the on-site brokers and directed them in their search for prospective tenants. I cultivated a large network of contacts with leasing brokers, tenant representatives, and building owners, which better enabled me to gauge market trends. Using the information synthesized from the marketplace, I was able to direct the leasing efforts and the strategy of the brokers and to manage the expectations of the project owner.

The Moscow State University where I got my undergraduate degree is known as the most prestigious and toughest school in the former USSR. Students at the Philological Department are often called "lead bottoms," because being very busy with their studies, they sit all day reading and do not have time for any extracurricular activities. I studied a lot too, but I was not very exited of getting that nickname and of missing an opportunity to participate in student social life, to meet many new people and to be a leader.

As I member of the Moscow State University Student Theater, I was the director, as well as one of the writers and actors, of a play performed at the annual department party where students and faculty meet alumni. The right to present the play at the party was awarded to the winners of the script competition. I convinced five of my friends to work with me on a script. After two weeks of intense writing we managed to assemble a script based on tales from Russian folklore. The script was judged by an elected committee. I was very excited when the dean announced that my team had won the competition.

Although we were awarded only 40% of our requested budget, we worked very hard to make our performance a quality production. We spent four weeks in rehearsal. I was extremely busy for I was not only the director and producer of the play, but also played one of the most important roles—a Mermaid. Not only did I have to learn my role, I also had to make sure that the twenty other people in the production showed up for rehearsals and learned their parts. At the same time that I was resolving these problems, I had to worry about costumes, scenery, playbills, my own role in the play and allocation of limited funds among competing yet equally important needs.

The most difficult part of the production involved a dance scene for which I needed to find a professional choreographer who was willing to work for my production without pay. In addition, recording the soundtrack also was something which needed professional involvement, but my friend managed to do it somehow.

Working on this production deeply affected my life. I discovered how exhilarating is to manage people. At first I worried that being responsible for so many aspects of a production—the actors, the script, choreography, the soundtrack, the lights, the stage—could be overwhelming. I had never worked on such a complex project before and I discovered during the production that I enjoyed the management aspects of my position even more than the artistic aspects. Also, having successfully directed such a project has provided me with greater confidence in positions I have had since that time.

As the culmination to my undergraduate career, I decided to embark on a challenging, yet exciting, endeavor: to write a development plan for a regional theater in metropolitan Detroit. The scope of this project demands that I use all of the knowledge and resources that I have gained through my work in both the academic and professional arenas.

I have spent numerous hours collecting and analyzing data. Through an analysis of the theater market in Detroit, I was able to show a significant "gap." Studying census data, community demographic information, and population projections, I have begun, with the help of the City of Detroit, to apply location theory to locate possible sites for the theater. Besides merely completing a market analysis and examining issues of location, the project also addresses the process of incorporation and nonprofit recognition, initial raising of capital and funds, organizational structure, the creation of a yearly budget, the hiring of a staff of theater artists and managers, the development of a production season, marketing, and actual production.

With a population of over seven million within 90 miles of the city, Detroit's lack of a professional regional theater to serve the entire metropolitan area is distressing. Theater is a powerful and necessary part of our society, and the opportunity to take part in a theatrical experience should be available to all, not just the elite or those living in the country's "theater centers." Theater not only serves as a source of entertainment, but also as a way of continuing education. As primary and secondary schools continue to cut the arts from their budgets, it is imperative that children gain exposure to the arts by alternative means. Numerous studies show the importance of the arts in the development and success of youth. The pedagogical qualities of theater, however, extend beyond their application to youth and pertain to adults as well by encouraging discussion and thought about societal issues and offering exposure to the diversity inherent in our society. A regional theater in Detroit is needed to fill a cultural void and encourage the growth of the arts and the region in general.

Despite the project's hypothetical intent, my goal in the end is to create a plan that could be realized. The opening of this theater is one of my greatest dreams; and with the completion of this plan, that dream is even closer to becoming reality.

Two years ago, I came to the Urban League of Eastern Massachusetts to volunteer my time to work in Boston's black community. As a social service organization, the Urban League is committed to seeing a better society. It provides a variety of different programs aimed at helping the community help itself. During my two years with the League, I have worked on and established several programs ranging from the Youth Leadership Program for neighborhood teenagers, to the Entrepreneur Incentive Committee aimed at encouraging minorities to become more involved in business, and to my current involvement as Committee Coordinator and mentor to adolescent fathers. My involvement in these programs has been sincere and committed to helping the community become a better place to live. I believe I offer the potential to develop into an active leader in the Boston business community. I want not only to establish a business here, but also to be responsible to the community in which I live and work. The Urban League has provided me with the opportunity to reach the community, and I believe that someday, I will provide opportunities for those same people who I am helping today.

What I consider to be my third most substantial accomplishment is the most important because it is a perpetual feat. I grew up in a predominantly black neighborhood of Dorchester, Massachusetts, but I was educated until grade nine in a white school system in a suburb of Boston. I was told when I was in sixth grade, after taking a standardized test in which I was asked to discern the English meaning of certain mumbled words in a fictitious language, that I would be unsuccessful at learning a foreign language, and that it would be best not to enroll in a language course in junior high school. In the seventh grade I enrolled in French; needless to say, I have since become fluent. In my sophomore year of high school, I enrolled in Spanish, and through my continued studies at Harvard, I have acquired a thorough command of the Spanish language. This year I enrolled in elementary Portuguese with the intention to continue my studies individually, post-graduation, in order to achieve a level of fluency comparable to that which I have achieved in Spanish and French.

During high school, I was challenged, motivated and encouraged to become a genuine achiever. Nevertheless, I was discouraged from applying to Harvard, although I was President of the School, would graduate third in my class, and received superior SAT, Achievement and Advanced Placement scores.

I have never let the lack of economic resources which pervaded in my family discourage me from attaining my goals, for I viewed the financial aspect of my endeavors as a formality which I could overcome by seeking out scholarship assistance from various organizations and donors. I have become a role model for many individuals in my community and in my family. Yet many have questioned my ability to overcome my economic restraints and succeed. I frequently receive comments such as: "who would have ever thought that a girl from Dorchester would be at Harvard?" Through my achievements and as a role model, I hope to make that "phenomenon" less of a shock and more of a normality.

EXTRACURRICULAR ESSAYS

What do you do when you're not at work?
Who cares?

B-schools care, and with good reason. A lot of the best ideas come to a business person in the shower or at the bowling alley. Your work is part of an interrelated whole, and what you do out of the office has an impact on what you can do on the job. Consider how your behavior in your personal life affects or reflects your business life.

This type of essay also can make you likeable. The business world can be harsh, and you need to show what kind of humanity you can bring to it. A recent study in the *New York Times* reported that humor among office workers increases productivity and stimulates creative thought. Quirky, interesting, and humorous people make work and school more exciting. And they can certainly make an application essay more readable.

If somebody had told me six months earlier that on a fall day in October I would be running in the Chicago marathon, I would have thought they were crazy. While I have always been a physically active person, running 26.2 miles would have seemed like a feat reserved for experienced athletes, not for someone like myself who jogged a mere three miles a few times a week. I never participated in any sports growing up; I focused instead on artistic and academic team activities, such as playing in the orchestra or competing on the high school speech team.

Nashville hosted its first marathon last spring and I was so inspired by the participation and dedication of thousands of people that I caught the "marathon bug" and decided to train. From a co-worker, I learned of the Galloway Program, a training regimen that claimed that running 26.2 miles could be fun, feasible, and injury-free. My first meeting was on a brisk Saturday morning in May. For some reason, I didn't fully grasp that this meeting was only the beginning of six long months of early Saturday mornings. There were about 60 people in the first meeting who encompassed all shapes, sizes and fitness levels. We were given our weekly training schedule and weekend mileage and placed into pace groups depending on our speed. I appreciated the discipline of the program and was motivated by both the noticeable results and camaraderie of the runners in my pace group. Because I was faithful to my weekly runs and cross training, I was able to add on mileage during the weekend. Before I knew it, I was able to run 10, 12, 18 miles, something I would never have thought myself capable of. My Saturday runs began earlier as the summer heat grew more intense. Though I often wondered what I was doing when my alarm went off at 4 A.M. on Saturday morning, I depended on the support of my running group. We helped each other get through the anxiety and doubting that we all faced before each long run.

I ran with my group Saturday morning, October 22 in Chicago. Crossing the finish line 5 hours and 39 minutes later, I felt an overwhelming sense of accomplishment. In addition to feeling physically stronger, I have also become more self-confident and approach challenges with a "can-do" attitude.

I was brought up in a family that was internationally oriented, and intellectually and culturally open and diverse. My father was Chairman of the Islamic Art Department at the Metropolitan Museum of Art in New York and a Professor at the Institute of Fine Arts of New York University. My mother is an archeologist specializing in Byzantine art and has participated in excavations in Turkey for the last eight years. I was encouraged from an early age to explore new subjects and modes of thought, and was exposed to diverse peoples and cultures on a regular basis. Friends of the family from around the world frequently visited our house. Even the decor of our house reflects the Middle East and Europe. When I had the chance to travel abroad, my experiences felt like an extension of the house in which I grew up. I travelled extensively throughout Europe and the Middle East. Eager to meet and exchange ideas with those I met, I actively learned foreign languages so as to better communicate and understand the countries and the peoples I was visiting. I am fluent in French and am proficient in German, Persian, and Arabic.

My curiosity about how people from foreign lands live and work also applies to people here in the United States. I have benefited greatly from the diverse experiences I have encountered in America. These many experiences have allowed me to cultivate a questioning and curious mind, and have enabled me to develop the ability to approach problems with a wide perspective. My experience as a volunteer fire-fighter, assistant ice hockey coach for [a day school's] varsity ice hockey team, sales coordinator for Sotheby's, and aircraft pilot gave me a breadth of experience not found in the "normal" college curriculum. Within the college community, I complemented my outside activities by working as Advertising Manager for *Nassau Weekly* and rowing on the Cornell and Princeton University crew teams.

One particular interest that has emerged from my background has been my interest in art. I believe that much can be understood from examining the artistic creations from a particular society. While my parents have imparted me with a strong background in the history of art and a particular understanding of the art of the Middle East, I have personally developed a fascination for American art of all periods and have a particular interest and expertise in American 18th century furniture. I derive a great deal of pleasure from this activity and find that my artistic sensibilities and art appreciation complement my other work.

My daughter's public school was suffering from a lack of leadership and enthusiasm. All but two of the eleven children in our immediate neighborhood had opted for private schools. As a PTA board member, I became aware of the principal's discouraging attitude toward his school population. When his remarks became negative toward latch-key children and Blacks, the board became motivated to seek help from the superintendent. We were able to petition the superintendent for a hearing. As a former teacher, I was asked by the board members to draft a position paper and present our allegations. As spokesperson at the hearing, I was able to convince the superintendent of the seriousness of the problem. Though the situation was a somewhat unpleasant one, the results for the community were positive. The school received a new principal. The parents became motivated. The PTA, which had never had enough money for basic supplies, undertook a campaign to fund new playground equipment. I organized an auction and we raised the $3000 necessary for our goal. My efforts in this situation demonstrate my ability to motivate others and to achieve goals.

If my personality is a continuously evolving sculpture, my parents' divorce wet the clay and three activities molded the basic structure. My parents' divorce created a confused, introspective child determined to prove himself. Working with these basic traits, religion, music, and athletics shaped my personality. Religion propelled me most to search for new thoughts. Playing the piano I discovered the excitement inspired by an insurmountable challenge and experienced the dynamics of a group experience. Rowing crew I tested my determination and strengthened my conviction that the most satisfying achievements result from team efforts. These three activities all had a significant impact on shaping my personality. Today, I am a determined, team-oriented individual who requires a constant challenge and seeks a diversity of ideas.

My parents separated when I was seven years old. At that age, the egocentric mind of a child attempts to explain the world in terms of himself. Somehow, I felt, I must have been an instigator of the irreconcilable problems between my parents. I could not otherwise understand how two people that I loved could not love each other. Confused about people's emotions, I distanced myself from my classmates and became introverted. Meanwhile, I was determined to reestablish the love that I thought I had marred with my parent's divorce. My mother's passion was religion; my father's was music. I assumed these two interests, probably expecting to reestablish my parents' love for each other. Of course, I did not realize how important these activities would become for my self-development.

Seeing the fervor with which my mother followed Catholicism, I eagerly explored many aspects of the faith. I was a devout Catholic. However, living in a very Jewish neighborhood, I was intrigued that many people happily espoused a different religion. My parents encouraged my curiosity, and occasionally I visited Hebrew School with my Jewish friends.

These afternoon visits left me perplexed about the disparity in beliefs. As I grew older, I launched into a study of philosophies to discover the presumptuous adolescent "truth." My search uncovered ideas I had never conceived of through Nietzsche, Buddhism, Sartre, and Zen. While clinging to my Catholic heritage, I could not resolve the potpourri of persuasive ideas I had encountered.

I spent my last two years of high school at Phillips Academy where I became actively involved in the school's Catholic organization, the Newman Club. The diversity of the student body and openness of the campus priest provided the final catalyst for me to develop a personal Christian religion. While earlier I had intellectualized religion, seeking a "right" answer, I now recognized there was no absolute right nor eternal wrong: no "best" way. There are only increasingly better ways, and these better ways are often realized through a synthesis of different approaches. Senior year, as president of the Newman Club, I was consulted by classmates to discuss problems or dilemmas. We discovered solutions together through honest appraisals of the alternatives, without depending on a pre-fabricated morality. Solutions are not easy without rigid, determined guidelines, but what may resolve one problem may merely aggravate another. Through religion I recognized the lack of absolutism, thereby establishing a need for fresh ideas and an open mind.

I started playing the piano at age eight and became serious about music at age thirteen, when I finally began to feel the music I was playing. Practicing for hours, I would revel in the mathematical precision of a Bach fugue or the wistful ardor of a Chopin nocturne. I felt excitement when a piece took form after weeks of labor, although I understood how much more could still be expressed by the notes. Music offered an exciting challenge that required dedication and provided a thrilling sense of satisfaction.

My musical interest expanded beyond solo performance with the discovery of chamber music, a new aspect of music. Flowing from the different players of an ensemble, a chamber music piece would establish its own will. Although each participant maintains his personality, all the members of the group work together, playing off each other, defining each other. This was the first time that I worked so closely with people. As a soloist one may admire or respect a different interpretation of a piece while maintaining an independent view. However, in chamber music the energies of the different ideas are incorporated into one body to inspire a piece with vitality. Chamber music sparked my interest in team-oriented goals.

Although I attended Yale largely because of its School of Music, as a freshman I realized that I did not have sufficient talent to establish a successful career in music. Yale had attracted pianists much more gifted than I. While I continued studying the piano throughout college and playing chamber music with friends, I decided to attempt a new challenge. I had never been athletic, but I wanted to participate on a collegiate team. I tried out for the Lightweight Crew. Although crew was known for intense physical demands, I also viewed it as an ultimate team sport.

Initially, the trial was not too difficult. We spent the afternoons practicing technique, only occasionally exerting ourselves. After Thanksgiving, we moved indoors, and the real test began. As intense workouts drove us to exhaustion, hopefuls dropped out. As teammates motivated each other through long practices, friendships formed among the survivors.

The crew became a team during Spring training in Florida. For two weeks we lived rowing. Although we competed for the same seats, camaraderie reached new highs. We all respected and trusted each other after the long trial period. Once the boats were set, the trust, loyalty and friendships consolidated during Florida would be critical for the success of the crew. During a race, when exhaustion and pain set in, testing my physical limitations, I continued knowing that my teammates were also pushing their hardest, also exhausted. We counted on each other, giving the most that we could give for ourselves and for the team. Through crew I learned how to depend on others and have others depend on me. At the end of Freshman year I received the first boat's MVP award, not for extraordinary physical prowess, but for spirit and determination. This award symbolized the rewards of everlasting friendships and self-confidence which a team sport offers.

Music and crew have imbued me with a love of challenges and taught me patience, determination, and the importance and satisfaction of working with people towards a common goal. Combining these qualities with a dynamic personal religion that leaves me restlessly searching for new ideas, I am still exploring myself and the world around me. My self-development is not over; the sculpture is far from complete.

Personal PERSONAL STATEMENTS

Business schools are not all business.

More than ever before, schools want to develop a class of individuals with solid values, committed either to family or to a familial community. Where did you come from? What did you learn along the road to B-school? What can you bring from your life experience that will be an advantage to this class, as well as to future employers or employees?

The MBA program is intense: two power-packed years that can result in a high-profile job and a starting pay that exceeds many other degree areas. The better schools want to know something more about what makes you tick, and a *personal* personal essay, one that reveals something about your family or your background, gives the admissions officers one more link to knowing who you really are.

The three essayists in this section represent different approaches and experiences, but each invites the reader into a private space, at least for the moment.

"The reality of life is that your perceptions—right or wrong—influence everything else you do. When you get a proper perspective of your perceptions, you may be surprised how many other things fall into place."

Was this really going to happen? An uneventful but pleasant dinner meal was abruptly suspended by the announcement that our family would soon move from our Charlotte home. I was numb with disbelief. While the thought of moving was itself disruptive enough, it was our destination that left me stunned. My father informed us that we would soon be leaving North Carolina and the United States to take up residence in Sydney, Australia.

From my parents' sanguine perspective, moving to Sydney represented the "personal and professional opportunity of a lifetime." As a fifteen-year-old high school sophomore, I held a contrary view. Nearing the end of my first year at West Charlotte High School, I was making friends, excelling in sports, and counting the days until my sixteenth birthday and the freedom of a driver's license. The thought of departing my native city left me devastated and heartbroken at first, fearful and angry later. I was utterly convinced that a ten thousand mile relocation would ruin my life. My desperate requests to remain in the US filled the next few weeks; but fighting, begging, and pleading failed to weaken my father's resolve. Finally, sad and bitter, I traveled with my family to the land down under.

After our arrival, the positive side of the "personal and professional opportunity of a lifetime" continued to be elusive. Friends and relatives were half a world away, warm June weather was replaced with cold and steady winter rain, there was to be no driving until age eighteen, and worst of all, our new school required uniforms. While common in many cultures, school uniforms seemed cruel and unusual punishment, even for a penal colony. Surely, the darkest day in the Antipodes was when my brother and I were forced to don our blazers, ties, boaters, and "school shoes," and venture off to the private school world of SCECGS Redlands. Daily attendance in this alien education system, where math was "maths," and sports were "sport," did little to lift my spirits. After two months in Sydney, I remained despondent.

Three months after our arrival, the ship carrying our furniture and belongings docked in Sydney, and life improved dramatically. A few nights in a familiar bed can change one's perspective, even when wearing a boater; and coincidentally, September in Sydney meant the start of spring sports and tryouts for the basketball team. Shortly after being named to my school's varsity level squad, my circle of friends increased, and my dissatisfaction soon changed to contentment. Australian culture, seemingly alien and peculiar at first, became familiar and agreeable, and rapidly things began to fall into place. My new perspective allowed me to appreciate and enjoy life in Sydney, a beautiful and enchanting city.

The expatriate experience was a blessing. I learned to value another culture, visited numerous foreign countries, and formed friendships that have lasted for a decade. Surely the most positive aspect of my fifteen-month sojourn in Australia was the recognition that a difficult life obstacle can, with effort, be seen as an incredible opportunity. Part of this paradigm shift was the realization that one's personal outlook and attitude is often more the issue than the obstacle itself.

When it came time for me to leave my family and return, alone, for my senior year at West Charlotte High School, I was again faced with an intimidating challenge. This time however, I was ready for the race, and cleared the first hurdle with ease. The first hurdle was not the actual difficulty of living away from my parents at age seventeen, but managing my own perceptions to recognize that any obstacle, no matter how great, can be overcome.

My family background has significantly shaped my values, ideals, interests and aspirations. From the age of six, I was raised in Greenwich, CT, an affluent and private town (Pop: 60,000), 45 minutes via car from New York City. Greenwich served all my needs: the public school system was excellent and challenged me to excel; town youth activities such as soccer and museum/nature/educational activities provided me an outlet for diversion and further stimulation, as well as the opportunity to make new friends; and the town's seclusion and privacy provided me the freedom (and provided my parents the comfort) to explore my surroundings and just be a kid. As a youngster and as a teenager, I was aware of the sheltered and privileged nature of my schools and town. Although my family lived comfortably, I was repeatedly exposed to conditions less favorable than mine as I explored substantially poorer regions during my parents' trips to Eastern Europe. Thus, I learned early to be thankful and mindful of my relatively easy and cozy life in Greenwich.

Yet, Greenwich was not always as idyllic a place as one would imagine. As one of the few Jewish students in a predominantly Christian public school, I often was the target of jokes or outright anti-Semitism. To this day, I remember the mixed feelings I had—hurt, fear, confusion, embarrassment, anger. At first, I tried to ignore it, put it behind me, like a bad day. Eventually, I discussed it with my parents. I came to understand that fears of racial, ethnic or religious differences—the unknown, the atypical, the unaccustomed—often guide actions; that ignorance is not an excuse; and that intolerance is often generation-oriented, handed down from old to young. I learned to keep an open mind, to delight in differences, to love and nudge the uninformed, and to be sensitive to diverse perspectives. I credit my parents with instilling these beliefs in all my interactions.

I credit my mother, an only child of Hungarian Jewish immigrant parents and an educator by training, with my relentless commitment to education. She taught me the art of intellectual discovery and, thus, gave me the gift of intellectual independence. Encouraged to read and explore, I flourished in learning about whatever caught my fancy. Worlds opened up for me beyond what was required in school. I sought out readings on the "topic of the day" and delighted in knowing the depths of the subject at hand. To this day, as I find myself intrigued by a topic—most recently, wine and vineyards—I relish the time spent immersed in new learning. My mother gave me a lifetime gift and I find myself often sharing with her my new discoveries. My mother also made my "responsibilities" clear. Attending Hebrew school two days a week for ten years was my job; observing a Kosher home was her and my father's job. Although I am not deeply religious today, I attribute many of my personal beliefs to my religious upbringing: family relationships are a gift worth treasuring and understanding; knowledge is gained in both the home and classroom; and acknowledging custom or culture, regardless if practiced, opens the mind to tolerance, reflection and practical knowledge.

As opposed to my mother's more traditional upbringing in Bridgeport, CT, my father learned life's lessons from the streets of the Bronx. Lost as a teenager in a tough neighborhood where his father passed away young and where his mother was mentally ill-equipped to provide him the necessary guidance and structure, he turned to the U.S. Marines for answers, and eventually, the brokerage industry for a living. For as long as I can remember, dad has been a true businessman—from his swagger to his demeanor to his policy of no nonsense. Thus, my relationship with him was and continues to be different, yet very special. My father, although not completely devoid of compassion, was and will always be simply a busy man, even if not really busy. His mind is always racing—easily distracted, yet at the same time, astonishingly focused and efficient. Although more personable, I am in this and other respects the mirror image of my father. As such, I have learned and continue to practice his best lessons: I challenge if even marginally confused, rather than simply nodding my head; likewise, I negotiate, mindful of compromise, when I feel treated unfairly; I make informed decisions, conditioned to probe further when the risks/rewards of a decision are not visually apparent; and I have learned that anger is destructive and achieves no meaningful gain. As a self-starter with little to no formal education, my dad was my hero and continues to be my idol. His hard work as a stock trader, bond broker and Senior Vice President of Investments during his 25 years in New York City earned him great admiration, skill, knowledge . . . and an early retirement at age 48. He is now a Professional Investor, as he calls it, for kicks. As my dad's examples (the value of hard work; being competent and reputable) began to pay off in my personal and academic life, I watched his every move. Dinner time conversation, where I had an otherwise always-engaged father's complete attention, sparked my interest in Wall Street. At the age of fifteen, I had my first formal foray to the world of stocks and bonds with a Fundamentals of Wall Street workshop hosted by New York University. Hooked early, I accompanied my father to the office often. Soon enough, I was a regular Summer Intern. Here I felt and touched the action. I thank my father for my professional passion; I credit him with a mentoring style that over time allowed freedom to explore, opportunity to experience, and time to commit.

My relationship with my younger brother (now 23), today a promising production coordinator at a large German multimedia/ entertainment company, was and continues to be equally rewarding. Though as children we were (and still are) diametric opposite personalities, today I am calmed and refreshed by his reserved and quiet manner. Respectful of our differing styles, we have grown closer as we have grown older. Currently, we share a mutual interest in technology and communication. Our conversations are respectively lively (my passionate, energetic, challenging style) and analytical (his objective, cautious style), culminating in an often surprising conclusion—agreement!

Perhaps the most vivid memory of my youth is being "dragged" from one art exhibition to another—museums, private galleries, auction houses. My parents are passionate for antiquities and avid collectors of 19th Century/Victorian/Pre-Raphaelite paintings and sculptures. As a result, today I also love, admire and collect art, particularly 19th Century European paintings. I am most fascinated by what is real and by that to which I can relate. For me, 19th Century European paintings reflect the realist tradition and exude the notion, "truth to nature." These paintings tell a story, connecting the observer to the subject's plight. Such pictures communicate to me life's hard facts, truths and opinions. They are tangible with clear messages that provoke analysis and thought.

The Kazakh Soviet Socialist Republic (now known as Kazakh-stan), where I was born, was home to people of many ethnic backgrounds in Soviet times. The Kazakhs are nomadic people of Mongol extraction, who embraced Islam in the 17th century. Some of the people of the Kazakhstan, like my maternal grandparents, came to Kazakhstan at the request of the Communist Party to help develop industry of the republic. Others were forcibly relocated, particularly during Stalin's reign.

I was brought up in a very international family, as my mother is half-Russian and half-Ukrainian and my father is Kazakh. As a child I was equally exposed to these three cultures. As every other kid of my age, I was admitted to a Pioneer youth organization and automatically became a granddaughter of Comrade Lenin. I remember how I commanded a frontier detachment at the school's annual military march and song competition dressed in a frontier troops uniform that my mother made for me from green paper.

After my parents divorced, my mother and I moved to West Siberia, for four years. We had no TV, no telephone, just a radio. On days when it was −60°F outside, the radio announced that schools were closed. It was a relief because at −30°F schools remained open. This region of Western Siberia is known for its oil resources and thousands of people work in oil extraction industries. The strongest impression from that time was from the volunteer work I performed at a local hospital. Every week, dozens of burned oil workers were brought into the hospital. You suddenly get much older when you see this.

When I finished high school in Siberia, I had to choose a university. Being ambitious and naïve, I decided to go to Moscow and apply to Russia's most prestigious school. The Philological Department at Moscow State University is known as one of the most difficult programs to get into in the whole former Soviet Union—unless you are the daughter of a diplomat or political leader. Despite my academic achievements in high school, in the fight for very limited space, I could not beat the Muscovite students who had received special preparation for the difficult entry exams. I was not accepted into the program, but decided to re-apply the next year.

Since I was not a Muscovite and did not have a residence permit stamp in my passport, I could not enroll in the free preparation course. So I worked in a library during the day and studied every night and every weekend for nine months. I could barely afford to pay a private tutor, but not much more. It is hard to believe now, but I had nothing to eat sometimes. That was the hardest period of my life, but at the same time it was the first major challenge of my life and I was rewarded in the end. I earned excellent marks on the entry exams and was admitted to Moscow State University's Philological Department.

During my five years at the university, I studied literature and linguistics, learned poems in Old Greek, read the Bible in Old Slavonic, learned Spanish, Polish and even some Khet, directed student theater performances, and played basketball. I enjoyed both my academic work and extracurricular activities. I had excellent teachers, and met most of my close friends at Moscow State University. I also gained an understanding of what is valuable in people: honesty, sincerity and loyalty.

The challenges I faced enabled me to develop a keen belief in myself, my independence, my ability to adapt to difficult situations, and my ability to learn quickly. I think that my experiences in Kazakhstan and Russia, my studies at Moscow State University, and my work experience will add to the diversity of perspective at The Fuqua School of Business. I look forward to contributing to student life at Fuqua, and to sharing my knowledge about the national traditions, literature and folklore of Russia and Kazakhstan.

OFFBEAT ESSAYS

As the title of this final section implies, these essays were very hard to fit into any one category. All of them, however, combine good writing, creativity, and a sense of vigor that is fun to read and meaningful.

The main problem with offbeat essays is that they can become gimmicky. High school seniors can sometimes get away with a quirky college application essay; business school applicants cannot. You'll never recover from an essay viewed as immature or silly, so be extremely careful with your offbeat idea. Note that the essays in this group used humor only to emphasize the more serious aspects of the writer's personality and goals.

The first piece begins like a novel or travelogue. By bringing us into the jungle, the writer captures our imagination and dramatizes the importance of her ecological interests. Her job in the New York Sanitation Department—a yawn at first glance—becomes part of an exciting theme.

The next essay describes the applicant in a lighthearted dialogue between admissions officers. By preempting potential criticism in an amusing manner, the writer builds his case without defensively lecturing or listing—two common mistakes.

The "retirement" speech shows farsightedness and ambition, and the minority essay tackles a ticklish controversy head-on. The next essay demonstrates an ability to solve a very specific problem, namely formulating an e-commerce strategy for a company in which the top-level employees are old-timers who have very little e-commerce experience. And the final three entries in this section all responded to the same topic: Write a newspaper article about yourself ten years after graduation.

Admissions officers say they don't "necessarily" want to be entertained by essays. But if you can give an experience or an idea a delightful twist, if you can demonstrate an ability to see things with a unique perspective, or if you can offer creative solutions to problems, then your readers will be with you all the way.

Red and blue macaws screeched across the sky. Monkeys chattered as they passed from tree to tree. A seven foot poisonous snake sunned itself on a branch at the river's edge. Thousands of leafcutter ants, each carrying a leaf ten times its size, formed a trail six inches wide.

During a river trip down a tributary of the Amazon last summer, I was awed by the natural bounty of Ecuador's tropical rain forest. The spectacular scenery was surpassed only by the diversity of species. According to some estimates, the Amazon Basin contains six million different plants, animals and insects, only a small fraction of which have been discovered and classified by scientists. Biologists, fearful that many species will disappear before they can be identified, have stepped up efforts to study them.

While western science is just beginning to comprehend the value of the tropical rain forest as a resource, the indigenous people have always found it rich in useful materials. Our guide sliced a piece of bark off a tree and explained that the Aucas used its slippery underside as a lubricant to dislodge canoes stuck on sand. He directed us to another tree which produced a substance used to heal wounds, one of 1300 medicinal plants known to the Indians of the Amazon.

Biological diversity in the tropical forest stems from the complexity of its ecosystem. After having us taste the lemon ants crawling inside a hollow branch of a nearby tree, our guide explained that the ants and the tree were interdependent. The tree provides the ants with a home and a source of food; the ants protect the tree from natural predators. Both have evolved in such a way that neither can live without the other. This pattern of symbiosis is repeated throughout the jungle, creating a diverse yet fragile environment.

Because of this fragility, it does not take much to upset the delicate natural balance of the tropical forest. Our guide told us that in six months the landscape before us would be changed forever. Ecuador's government, already pumping 210,000 gallons of oil out of the jungle every month, planned to expand production to improve the country's financial situation. The proposed new wells would encroach on the rapidly shrinking boundaries of the virgin forest. The noise from the heavy machinery alone would drive the animals from the region completely.

I could empathize with the reasons behind the government's decision to exploit the tropical forest's short-term potential. My travels around Ecuador made me acutely aware of the need to generate capital and raise the standard of living of its people. Even if Ecuador recognized the long-term value of preserving the tropical forest, it could not afford to lose present oil revenue. In Quito, I watched students go on strike when the bus fare went up from 2 to 3 cents. In the Andean highlands, I visited villages which had no potable water and infant mortality rates of eighty-five percent. At this time, the tropical forest's raw materials provide Ecuador with its best hope for a brighter economic future.

Unfortunately, many of the tropical forest's resources are nonrenewable and their disappearance will have serious global consequences. Each year, 25,000 square miles of tropical forests are cleared by developing countries worldwide. In the process, thousands of species are lost. This translates into the greatest rate of species extinction since the dinosaurs vanished from the earth 65 million years ago. We cannot begin to calculate the loss because we do not know exactly what we are losing. What we do know is that the tropical forest has produced drugs to treat Hodgkin's disease and leukemia, germoplasm to revitalize crops, and the most prolific plant foods on earth.

Tropical forests face destruction because they are undervalued as resources. The international scientific community, which vocally supports the preservation of the earth's biological diversity, has only recently recast the plight of the rain forest in economic terms. Biologists now argue that the study of unknown plants and animals of the tropical forest will lead to agricultural and pharmaceutical applications to benefit all humankind. It is in our self-interest to preserve the earth's tropical forests and it is our responsibility to ensure their biological diversity. We have to begin to think about tropical forests in new ways.

Changing the way society values a resource is a difficult task. People often have to feel the direct impact of a crisis to alter their behavior. As an undergraduate, I encountered this in my study of the New Haven water supply at the turn of the century. Although the health risks of impure water were known and the technological means of purification had been developed, the people of New Haven did not demand filtration of their water supply until a typhoid epidemic claimed the lives of 51 residents. Only after New Haven experienced the tragedy of water-borne disease first hand were its citizens willing to pay the price of keeping their water pure.

People tend to respond resoundingly in the face of a crisis. Unfortunately, if we must wait until people feel the direct impact of the tropical forest's disappearance, there will not be much left to save. Nevertheless, my experience has shown me that there are other ways to make people change their behavior.

Only a short while ago, few people considered the Fresh Kills waste disposal site on Staten Island in New York City a resource, let alone a valuable commodity. The price to dump at the landfill was low, reflecting its perceived worth. No attempt was made to regulate the volume of New York City's waste. Some city managers recognized that Fresh Kills had a finite capacity and that other landfill sites or methods of disposal would have to be found. They proposed a technological solution: building resource recovery plants to burn garbage for energy. What these city managers did not foresee was the public resistance to the plants they intended to build. Nor did they anticipate the scope of the problem.

Throughout the Northeast, as environmental regulations have grown more stringent and the value of land has increased, towns and cities have run out of places to put their garbage. Few have developed replacement facilities such as resource recovery plants or have significantly reduced the volume of their waste through recycling. Therefore, they have had to pay steep prices to export their garbage to available landfills in distant counties and states. Unless these municipalities develop innovative solutions to their waste disposal problems, the situation will only get worse.

Many towns and cities in the Northeast face garbage crises because they have failed to assign the appropriate cost to waste disposal. As an analyst for the New York City Department of Sanitation, I am helping the City attempt to avoid the same mistakes by changing its waste disposal pricing policies while the City still has landfill space. We use an economic model to capture the present and future costs of operating New York City's entire waste disposal system and we base our rates on marginal pricing principles. These principles use the highest cost facility in the system to define the base rate. These rates set an efficient price for disposal, encourage recycling and provide incentives to private industry to develop new methods of waste disposal.

Although we have generated over 60 million dollars in annual revenue through dump fees, we have not yet realized our goal of diverting tonnage from the landfill. We have failed for a variety of reasons. In spite of the fact that we have raised our fees to unprecedented levels, we still charge rates at our landfill which fall below the true cost of waste disposal. My economic analysis dictates that we immediately raise our rates to reflect the cost of disposing the last ton. We have instead adopted a more gradual price increase to avoid shocking the system and give the commercial waste haulers some time to adjust to our new strategy. Furthermore, the money generated by dump fees goes into the City's general fund. If this money were earmarked to develop markets for recycled products, we might experience reductions in tonnage. The political considerations which have kept our rates artificially low and diverted money from recycling have cost the City valuable landfill space.

New York City's attempt to use price to preserve its landfill space provides a useful tool to examine the management of natural resources. There may be lessons for Ecuador in New York's experience. Marginal pricing which assigns depletion costs to non-renewable uses of resources could theoretically preserve the tropical forest. It could also pay for the costs of preservation by generating revenue from an international base of users such as pharmaceutical and chemical companies who benefit directly from the forest's products. Marginal pricing offers no guarantee that the tropical forest, like New York City's remaining landfill, will be preserved but, accompanied by political commitment, it promises some real hope.

My experience in city government has given me insight into methods to preserve natural resources. It has also shown me that successful policy cannot be sustained on the basis of correct analysis alone. Decision-makers must be guided by political will and vision. My goal is to achieve a position in which I can take the lead in determining how natural resources are allocated based on respect for the environment, sound economics, and an awareness of future consequences.

To answer UCLA's direction to "Write your own essay question and answer it. Take a risk," one candidate did the following:

How would Bob and Jane, two esteemed members of the UCLA Admissions staff, discuss MBA candidate Bill Johnson's application for admission? Bob is against admission. Jane wants to accept him. (Any resemblence to actual persons or events is purely coincidental and should not be held against the applicant.)

Bob: O.K. Jane, I've looked at Johnson's file and frankly, I've got my doubts.

Jane: Bob, get serious. We've got to accept this kid. Give me specifics—if you don't want him, tell me exactly why.

Bob: For starters, his GMAT score is mediocre.*

Jane: You think a silly test tells you anything about anybody? Johnson's always tested very averagely. Andover and Princeton accepted him despite his mediocre SSAT and SAT scores. I mean a 560/620 on the SAT must be 200 or so points below the Princeton average. Yet look at his academic record there: graduated cum laude in history, got

---

* This is an assumption. I took the test in January.

an A− on a unique Senior Thesis, and received A's on his Junior Independent work. This is a very bright kid.

Bob: All right, but he's a little young; he doesn't have enough experience to really take advantage of our program.

Jane: I was just about to get to that. Do you want pizza or Chinese tonight? Pizza? Good. At least we can agree on something. Call up Domino's while I lecture you on Johnson's experience. He's written advertisements that have appeared in *Time*, *Esquire*, and *Glamour* among other national publications. He supervised a direct mail operation that raised $2,000,000. The Zschau campaign was the largest federal election campaign in the United States, the second most expensive in the history of the country and Johnson was a part of it. On the campaign, he was given goals and he exceeded them; he's met deadlines, knows how to communicate to a variety of markets across the country, understands budgets and has worked carefully with numbers. Direct mail is dependent on accurate interpretation of the returns, so that you can predict things like yield, rate per piece mailed, cost per piece mailed . . . so that you can learn how often to mail and to whom. I think he's done an awful lot in a short amount of time.

Bob: I don't know, doesn't seem like he's taken any risks.

Jane: You've got no case here. As most of his Princeton pals were interviewing for jobs on Wall Street, Johnson took a chance and moved to California. I think that shows a lot of initiative—I mean, all of his friends, his family, were in the East. When he joined the campaign, Zschau didn't even register in the polls. Either Johnson was crazy or he seized upon a unique opportunity. I subscribe to the latter.

Bob: Well, I subscribe to magazines.

Jane: Admit it, we should let him in—he's a go-getter, he's smart, his recommendations are strong, he's motivated and he's had unique and solid experiences. Oh good, the pizza arrived.

Bob: Ahhh . . . mushrooms and pepperoni.

Jane: You know I hate mushrooms.

Bob: Yup.

The topic: "Write your retirement speech." Here's how one applicant handled it:

Members of Congress, distinguished guests, ladies and gentlemen, members of the press, I thank you for spending an evening seeing this old codger off. Now that the coffee is poured, sit back and endure the reminiscings of a man about to spend three months sailing on a boat no larger than the cubicle assigned him in his first job as analyst at an investment bank called Salomon Brothers. (You know it better as the merchant bank Salomon, Sumitomo and Sons.) Well, there have been more offices than I dare count since then. But throughout my career, if there was one thing I could count on, it has been the continuing internationalization of the world's economy. I suppose that's why I've had so many offices!

Shuttling between private industry, supranational agencies and government positions—as I and most of you here have done—is a requirement of a world where few transactions fail to touch all three of these sectors. Before assuming my present position in the State Department, I was, as you know, managing partner of an international economic consulting firm. Our firm encountered numerous companies—in both service and manufacturing—that failed financially because they dealt ineffectively with (or worse, ignored) one or more of these cornerstones of the world's economy.

133

Now I never thought I'd learn Korean, or wine and dine government bureaucrats in Eastern Mongolia, or prepare an annual report in North American Currency Units—but I've done it all and more these past thirty years. In fact, the three examples I just gave were all required to complete a series of manufacturing and trade agreements for a supra-tech company I used to manage. I arranged for one of our products—designed by my company here in the States—to be manufactured in Mongolia and imported through a Korean import-export firm to the ever-growing markets of that country. All parties demanded that company financials be reported in the common language of NACUs. I complied with many (but not all) requests and signed agreements that still provide profits for everyone involved.

If asked to put my finger on the reason why I have been successful at working with and in such varied institutional and economic climates, I'd say I was fortunate in having a strong educational foundation from which to launch my career. A small liberal arts college in Massachusetts and a larger business school farther inland provided that foundation by instilling in me the necessity of adapting one's strategy to different environments—whether when reading a novel by Joseph Conrad or analyzing the economy of a third-world nation. Few situations render themselves accessible to standard strategies. Besides, who can agree on what constitutes these standard strategies?

Well, we can all probably agree on what constitutes a too-long speech so I'll close with an invitation to any of you sailors here tonight to sail along with me for a spell and chat some more about these and future times.

(This essay question asked the applicant to write as his company's new CEO.)

Considering the research projections that electronic commerce revenues will soon grow to nearly $1 trillion, we must consider our entrance into e-business. The economic volatility of many e-based businesses, however, dictates that we proceed with caution. We must weigh the prospects of each of our product lines, based on the success of our competitors, against the risks of investing in an e-commerce strategy.

Our Internet device competitors have established themselves in the e-marketplace and spent heavily to get there. Nevertheless, sales of their products through traditional retail channels still far outweigh their e-commerce revenues. Sizeable investment in virtual storefronts and web hosting has, as of yet, yielded minimal return. Similarly, our MP3 player competition has adopted an aggressive spending strategy that appears distant from e-commerce profitability.

In contrast, our double-digit growth continues to surprise the analysts. Maintaining our informative, customer-friendly web site has not been costly, and has allowed us to remain focused on our presently successful business strategy. Currently, our distribution channels are well established, our branding initiatives have been successful, and our management team is thriving, though each of these elements is mature.

Entering the more volatile e-commerce arena could severely disrupt the cohesion of our senior level employees, including Murphy and Kline. Their contributions to this point have been immense, but they have been slow to follow web-based developments. If we proceed with an e-business strategy, we must provide the entire management team with adequate preparation and training, since these individuals will continue to define our success in the future.

Considering all these factors, keeping pace with external change means that we must, to some extent, initiate an e-business plan. Selling our Internet access devices and MP3 players online is an inevitable part of the future, and we must begin the transition process. For now, we should focus primarily on existing market intermediaries to sell these product lines. As the market evolves, a dedicated online store could augment this growth. Consumer purchasing of Internet access devices will continue to increase steadily, but we should be alert to the sensitive and changing environment surrounding MP3's. Our MP3 strategy needs to be nimble. For both product lines, the strength of our bricks and mortar network can serve as a competitive advantage, allowing us to leverage easy return policies as an online buying bonus, though I understand there are some state tax issues.

Perhaps our most significant opportunity, however, lies in the home appliance market. Growth here is less rapid than in other areas, but white goods still account for over fifty percent of our total revenues. Sales are consistent, our brand is well known, and product performance and reliability ratings are outstanding. Further, while Maytag and GE have functional Web sites in place, their marketing efforts have been ineffective; and failure to provide price advantage has led to disappointing online sales. Appliances may be relatively "low-tech" items, but they are universally common and feature variability is low.

We must not ignore this opportunity. High success rates have occurred when e-businesses can provide products with a known level of quality with an improvement in either price or convenience. We should be able to adapt our existing distribution channels and ship directly to consumers, thereby increasing our market share with minimal impact to profit margins. This could allow us to offer significant price savings to online shoppers, providing a major competitive advantage.

After having assessed the strategic considerations of preparing for e-commerce, we must then decide whether to implement the plan ourselves or rely on experts. Again considering that Murphy, Kline, and other management team members have minimal e-commerce experience, outsourcing non-strategic functions will allow us to focus on our core strategies of product design and manufacturing. IBM, EDS, and other e-business solution providers will bid down the price of an e-commerce implementation. Effective outsourcing should accommodate web store design, web hosting, payment solutions, and call centers, freeing us from these non-integral and unfamiliar tasks. An outsourced solution will provide the exact technology we need to accomplish our objectives, save us from wasting time and money, and get us quickly to market.

Both strategic and implementation issues must be addressed in a thorough analysis. While the growth of e-commerce is enticing for our business, we must be thoughtful in our approach, careful not to abandon our formula for success and the internal values of our company. In summary, we should use existing e-market intermediaries to make our Internet access devices and MP3 players available on the Web, and focus our efforts on the underdeveloped opportunities in the Home Appliance sector. We need to retain and preserve our management team, and give them training and incentives to maintain current productivity and profitability. No longer a choice, e-business is a necessary step to compete in the new economy. I will meet with my senior executives to get this initiative underway.

*(The topic: Write an article about yourself
ten years after graduation from business school.)*

BUSINESS LEADER BRINGS
"CAN DO" MESSAGE TO THE UK

As 23 bright-eyed 6th graders from the Notting Hill Preparatory School look on, Paula White moves about on stage with the enthusiasm of a prep school student herself, preaching her message on the power of positive thinking. But this is not just your ordinary "you can do anything if you put your mind to it" discourse. Each One Reach One is a creative motivational program that inspires disadvantaged young people to reach for success in business. Different from other student-oriented programs, Each One Reach One offers more than just the occasional pep talk. It is a comprehensive program that includes business education, mentoring, junior corporate internships, and college camps. The program, initially targeted towards young minorities and women, has expanded to include all youth who lack the skills and opportunities required for success in the global business community.

Paula White, 45, founder of Each One Reach One, uses her own life as example of the proverbial rags to riches story. Raised in inner city Detroit, White overcame socioeconomic and educational disadvantages to earn degrees both at West Point and Cox School of Business. "I always wanted to be successful," says White, "but not just for the sake of having success. I knew that I wanted to make a real difference in the community. Once I got back into the business sector after completing my MBA, I immediately searched for ways to help other young women and minorities achieve in business." White was able to use her contacts in the business community to obtain corporate sponsorships, and Each One Reach One was born.

It was during her visits to the UK while serving as an International Business Development Manager for Johnson and Johnson that White felt the urging to take the program across the Atlantic. "I realized that young people are disenfranchised everywhere. The Each One Reach One message is universal, and I'm thrilled to have the chance to share it with young people outside of the U.S."

(The topic: Write an article about yourself ten years after graduation from business school.)

WORKING WOMAN MAGAZINE

Engineer, author, professor, philanthropist, community activist, entrepreneur, entertainer, speaker. Is this a listing of possible career paths a college student may pursue? Yes, but it is also a listing of actual career paths our feature business woman has pursued. Dr. Desireè H. Young has proven to be a jack of all trades as well as a master of some. Her newest best seller *To Learn Better Is to Work Better* is sweeping the world as an entrepreneur's handbook, student's textbook, and business person's must-read. She has developed and facilitated workshops from Capitol Hill to storefront churches. As an activist, Dr. Young started a foundation that has placed centers in communities to benefit economic and people development. This feat has been accomplished by putting together an interesting combination of the nation's elderly, whom Dr. Young calls an untapped population of rich resources, and the nation's youth. She has been a consultant to the U.N. This work focused on developing cultural competence to establish business opportunities with areas such as the Sudan, which only 10 years ago was suffering from some of the world's worst cases of AIDS epidemics. As a professor, Dr. Young's courses are usually filled to capacity before the semester starts. She purposely keeps her classes small to hone a hands-on approach rather than just a lecture. Dr. Young's oral exam technique is used so that students can prove the understanding and application of the material. One of Young's students states, "Dr. Young is challenging but prepares you for the real world. I got as much out of her class as I did in my internship."

One could say that Dr. Young was destined for success at an early age. Her first public speech was at the tender age of seven in her local church. Through dedication and perseverance, she finished first in her high school class and was deemed student of the year by her home state Louisiana. Torn with the decision to study communications or engineering, Dr. Young chose engineering because she thought it would challenge and stretch her abilities. She went on to finish her mechanical engineering degree from Boston University and then worked in a chemical plant as an engineer and training and development coordinator for six years. "One of the major turning points in my life was when two other friends and I had a weekend long 'career search' session. We discussed what we enjoyed doing, what we would like to do and the best way to get there. My list was probably the most varied in that it combined technology, business, and the arts. I just believed, however, that God would permit me to live long enough to pursue all of these things." She later received her M.B.A. from the Cox School of Business in Dallas, Texas. If the career search weekend was a turning point, then attending Cox was certainly the catalyst that made her dreams realities. "Although challenging, Cox taught me how to see myself as a company that had lots of products to market. My main venture however, like Cox, was to invest in others so that they can be successful businesses or people." Based on opportunities gained at Cox, Young worked internationally for three years in organizational development and strategic consulting, pursued her Ph.D. in the same field and started her own consulting business. Based on her drive and life's philosophy, this is one woman who will no doubt be around a long time.

*(The topic: Write an article about yourself
ten years after graduation from business school.)*

PERSONAL PROFILES: JONATHAN JAMESON

INTRASTAT MAGAZINE:
The International Strategic Manager's Magazine

Lounging by the side of the pool at his spacious home is a man who is no stranger to success. Mention his name to any international consulting firm and heads pop to attention like soldiers on the first day of boot camp. Mention his name to a university and Palm Pilots flip open to take notes. What is all the fuss about? Jonathan Jameson—strategic planning expert, corporate culture designer, and organizational change guru.

One would expect to encounter a powerful personality upon meeting him, but his soft-spoken, friendly disposition erases all fears. Responding to the question of what is on his mind, Jameson delves into a humorous tale about the latest family gathering and shares his excitement about an upcoming church retreat. No mention of stocks, speaking engagements, not anything career related. "It's the weekend!" he laughs.

If anyone deserves a peaceful weekend, Jameson is the one. After earning his MBA at the Fuqua School of Business at Duke University, Jameson joined an organizational change consulting firm where his knack for designing some of the best training and recruiting programs did not go unnoticed. Feeding his love for traveling and utilizing his Spanish fluency, Jameson circled the globe, advising companies on issues ranging from ethics to cultural sensitivity to the sociological impact of technology in the third world. While home, he offers pro-bono consulting services to up-and-coming entrepreneurs in disadvantaged areas.

When not toiling so hard, Jameson lets his fingers dance around the grand black and white keys, writing songs, hoping some pop star turns at least one of them into a hit (a lifelong dream of his). As a children's book author, he fires up his uncanny humor to impart values and self esteem. "They've got ideas we haven't dreamed of yet." As for his own future, Jameson ponders the idea of entering academia, but he says he enjoys life as it is at the moment.

SOME FINAL ADVICE FROM A TEAM
OF *Business Week* EDITORS

The advice and examples in this book demonstrate the importance of the business school application essay and the best ways to write an effective one. *Business Week* editors agree that the essay needs to be outstanding. Note the following excerpts from their essay, "Crafting the Perfect B-school Essay" in the book *Business Week Guide to the Best Business Schools* (McGraw-Hill):

> *The B-school essay questions are your single best opportunity to make yourself really shine for an admissions staff. Yet they can just as easily be your downfall if you drown your responses in clichés and bland, nonspecific examples, says Jon Megibow, admissions director at the University of Virginia's Darden Graduate School of Business Administration. "Getting four essays that deal with nothing but platitudes and content that answers what we want to hear is counterproductive. The essays are an opportunity to display the different facets of the applicant's character."*

Remember, when answering the essay questions, be sure to emphasize how different you are, not only how great you are. "Don't view your essay as an academic article or a business memo, but as a human interest story about yourself," advises Linda Abraham, a consultant.

It's not enough to write about leading a project team or managing people of diverse backgrounds; you also need to discuss how you dealt with someone who didn't accept or respect you. . . . Sensitive to criticisms that MBAs are too self-centered, many schools today emphasize teamwork and read essays with an eye toward ferreting out the ego-maniacs. Says Donald P. Jacobs, dean of Kellogg, "We don't want loners with sharp elbows."

"If the school feels any part of the application is not the student's own work, they are immediately disqualified," says Robert Alig, Wharton's former director of admissions and financial aid. Alig's comment underscores a simple and very important point: Above all, honesty is vital.

ESSAY *News*

ESSAY *Advice*

ESSAY *Reviews*

ESSAY *Help*

www.essaysthatworked.com